Teaching Students to
Read Nonfiction

···················· **GRADES 2–4** ····················

20 Easy Lessons With Color Transparencies, High-Interest Passages,
and Practice Pages—Everything You Need to Help Your Students Learn
How to Read All Kinds of Nonfiction

by Alice Boynton and Wiley Blevins

New York • Toronto • London • Auckland • Sydney
Mexico City • New Delhi • Hong Kong • Buenos Aires

Teaching *Resources*

Text Credits Jokes from TEACHERS JOKES, QUOTES AND ANECDOTES edited by Patrick Regan, published by Andrews, McMeel Publishing. Copyright © 2001 by Andrews McMeel Publishing. Jokes from LITTLE GIANT BOOK OF SCHOOL JOKES edited by Charles Keller, published by Sterling Publishing Co. Copyright© 2000 by Charles Keller. "Wagon Trail Diary" and "The Great Migration" from COMMUNITIES: ADVENTURES IN TIME AND SPACE. Copyright © 1997 by Macmillan/McGraw Hill. "A Day on Mars" and "Reading Mars Info" from Spacekids presented by space.com. From THREE FABLES retold by Maryann Dobeck. Copyright © 2002 by Scholastic Inc. Reprinted by permission of Scholastic Inc. From STEP-BY-STEP GEOGRAPHY MAPS AND GLOBES BY Sabrina Crewe. Copyright © 1996 by Franklin Watts. Reprinted by permission of Children's Press, an imprint of Scholastic Library Publishing. "Stopping a Toppling Tower" from SUPERSCIENCE, Nov/Dec 1998. Copyright © 1998 by Scholastic Inc. Reprinted by permission. "Penguins" "Polar Bears" and "A Century of Hits" from SCHOLASTIC LITERACY PLACE. Copyright © by Scholastic Inc. Reprinted by permission. "Space Suit" from ESSENTIAL CONCEPTS EARTH SCIENCE CARD 25, Grade 3. Copyright © by Scholastic Inc. Reprinted by permission. "Living in Space" "Weather Watch" "The U.S. Welcomes Latinos" "Meet Gary Soto" "My Millennium Time Line" are reprinted from SCHOLASTIC NEWS. Copyright © 1998, 1998, 2000 and 2001 by Scholastic Inc. Reprinted by permission. "How a Butterfly Grows" from BUTTERFLY by Susan Canizares. Copyright © 1998 by Scholastic Inc. Reprinted by permission. "How Amphibians Grow and Change" from Grade 3 ESSENTIAL CONCEPTS LIFE SCIENCE CARD. Copyright © by Scholastic Inc. Reprinted by permission. "The Oregon Trail" and "Iroquois Communities" from ESSENTIAL CONCEPTS SOCIAL STUDIES CARDS, Grade 3. Copyright © by Scholastic Inc. Reprinted by permission. "Sounds All Around" and "What Makes a Sound" from SCIENCE PLACE. Copyright © 1995, 1997 by Scholastic Inc. Reprinted by permission.

Art Credits Page 8: fiction book illustration from THREE FABLES, retold by Maryann Dobeck, illustrated by Diane Dawson Hearn, © 2002 by Scholastic Inc.; nonfiction book illustration from MAPS AND GLOBES by Sabrina Crewe, illustrated by Raymond Turvey and Shirley Tourret, © 1996 Franklin Watts, first American edition 1997 by Children's Press, an imprint of Scholastic Library Publishing; page 57: photograph (l.) © Randy Wells/CORBIS; photograph (r.) © George D Lepp/ CORBIS; p. 61: photograph © Photodisc; pp. 66-67: Ms. Frizzle illustration by Bruce Degen from THE MAGIC SCHOOL BUS LOST IN THE SOLAR SYSTEM by Joanna Cole. Copyright ©1989 by Bruce Degen. All rights reserved. Used by permission of Scholastic Inc. Ms. Frizzle and THE MAGIC SCHOOL BUS are registered trademarks of Scholastic Inc; images of space @ NASA; p. 76: photographs (top to bottom), © AP/Wide World; © Dean Conger; AP/Wide World; p. 77: map, Jim McMahon, Scholastic Inc.; p. 91: photograph, © Greg Smith/Saba/CORBIS; p. 96: photograph of Gary Soto, © George Olson; p. 101: Peter Rabbit, © Penguin Publishing; Batman, © DC Comics; Amelia Bedelia, © Harper Collins Publishing; Clifford, from CLIFFORD, THE BIG RED DOG by Norman Bridwell. Copyright © 2003, 1964 by Norman Bridwell. All rights reserved. Used by permission of Scholastic Inc., CLIFFORD is a registered trademark of Norman Bridwell; Ms. Frizzle illustration by Bruce Degen from THE MAGIC SCHOOL BUS LOST IN THE SOLAR SYSTEM by Joanna Cole. Copyright © 1989 by Bruce Degen. All rights reserved. Used by permission of Scholastic Inc. Ms. Frizzle and THE MAGIC SCHOOL BUS are registered trademarks of Scholastic Inc; Julian, © Random House Publishing; p. 111: top photograph © James L. Amos/ CORBIS; p. 116: photograph (l.) © Craig Aurness/CORBIS; photograph (r.) © James L Amos/CORBIS; p. 117: photograph, © Museum of History and Industry/ CORBIS; p. 131: photograph, David S. Waitz for Scholastic Inc.; illustrations by Lynn O'Kelley; p. 136: photograph (top), Ken Karp for Scholastic Inc; p. 137: illustration, Lynne Prentice; p. 141: photograph (l.) © Nathan Benn/CORBIS; photograph (r.) Werner Furman Collection/CORBIS; p. 146: photographs (top to bottom), © The Schomburg Center for Research in Black Culture/ NYPL; © Brown Brothers, Sterling, PA; © Underwood & Underwood; p. 167: photograph of Jacob Lawrence, © Christopher Felver/CORBIS; painting by Jacob Lawrence, © Geoffrey Clements/ CORBIS.

Every effort has been made to acquire permission to use the materials in this book.

Cover design by Josue Castilleja
Cover images: photograph of two girls by David S. Waitz for Scholastic Inc.; vocal cords illustrations by Lynn O'Kelley; map by Jim McMahon, Scholastic Inc.; photograph of space suit © Photodisc.
Interior design by Sarah Morrow and Sydney Wright
Illustrations on pages 6, 11, 19, 23, 25 and 31 by Mike Moran

Contents

Introduction

For many readers—including us—nonfiction is a gateway to new ideas and unfamiliar territory. We feel a bit like Dorothy in the *Wizard of Oz* leaving her ordinary black-and-white world and stepping into a technicolor world filled with fascination and wonder. Some consider fiction a magic carpet ride. But for us, nonfiction is the vehicle, and all the more exciting because what we're reading about is true; it really happened! It is hard for us to imagine not knowing about Cleopatra and her fate with the slithering asp, not learning about how Abraham Lincoln made our country a more civil and fair society, or not discovering the magic behind a fuzzy caterpillar turning into a delicate and beautiful butterfly.

Nonfiction has transported us to worlds old and new, filled our heads with information that has enriched our lives, and helped us survive in today's technologically-advanced world. Francis Bacon stated, "Knowledge is power." As teachers, we are constantly searching for ways to give our students the tools that will enable them to be successful. Teaching students to navigate, read, and comprehend nonfiction text not only gives them the information they need, it also gives them an avenue for exploring interests and satisfying their personal needs and desires. Knowledge *is* power! And, we have the mandate to give that power to each and every one of our students.

Alice Boynton

Wiley B

Nonfiction Survival Guide

Nonfiction—What Is It?

This may seem like an easy question. But, what really is nonfiction? Nonfiction, also called expository text, provides information. Its purpose is to explain, inform, or persuade. You may be surprised by how much non-fiction surrounds us every day—newspapers, subway maps, instructions for changing a vacuum cleaner bag, recipes, and the dreaded VCR manual. Teaching students to read nonfiction, therefore, is essential as we teach them to develop as readers.

It is widely quoted that in grades 4 through 6, the emphasis changes from learning to read to reading to learn. However, learning to read in the content areas begins in the primary grades. Young children can learn through text. And since research shows that being able to learn from text takes many exposures (Olson and Gee 1991), rich experiences in the primary grades provide children with a firm foundation for the more difficult materials they will face as they move up through the grades.

For some time, it was steadfastly maintained that children prefer story-books to other genres, such as information books. However, recent research has challenged this long-held belief. In a study of the books first graders selected during recreational reading time, it was found that many of the children showed a preference for information books (Donovan, Smolkin, and Lomax, 2000; Caswell and Duke, 1998).

Even kindergarten children have demonstrated a strong interest in information books. A study that tested kindergartners' ability to retell both information books and storybooks (Pappas, 1993) found that many of the children in the study preferred the information books to the storybooks. And, in their retellings, the kindergarten children who heard information books read aloud frequently from September to December incorporated more and more of the linguistic features of those books over time.

These findings don't suggest that the major focus in the elementary grades should be nonfiction. What they do reveal is that children in the early grades have a strong interest in information text, and that an elementary-grade classroom should include a balance of genres. Young children, therefore, already have the motivation to read and hear nonfiction. This makes the teacher's task of providing a firm foundation for learning from nonfiction materials that much easier. It also better prepares the child for the shift in the materials they will read in later grades.

As students progress through school, more and more of their reading is done in nonfiction, or expository, materials—content area textbooks, reference books, periodicals, and informative articles on the Internet, for example. The purpose for reading these texts is to acquire information. Unlike narrative text, which tells a story, expository text explains facts and concepts, many of them complex and difficult to understand. Expository materials differ significantly from narratives, and they pose many challenges to the student.

Why Is It Challenging?

Content

Reading and understanding expository text requires a high level of abstract thinking. Readers are called on not only to comprehend ideas that may be difficult, but also to extrapolate and remember the significant main ideas and to integrate them with other information from their prior knowledge. Students must be able to recognize complex causes and effects, compare and contrast ideas, synthesize information from a variety of sources, and evaluate proposed solutions to problems as they read. This is tough work for developing readers!

Vocabulary

Another major difference between narrative and expository text is the vocabulary that the reader encounters. Each content area has its own

Typical fiction page

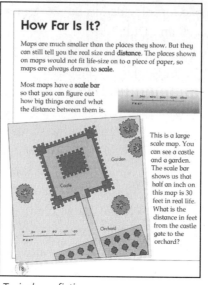

Typical nonfiction page

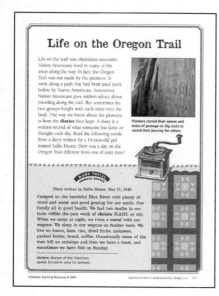

This text is clearly written with signal words, the text features are appropriately placed, the text is logically organized and not visually overwhelming.

specialized terms that students do not come up against in stories—or in conversation, either. Many of these terms are polysyllabic words that are more difficult to decode and pronounce. Here are some examples from typical science and social studies textbooks: *metamorphosis, photosynthesis, vibrations, transcontinental, artifacts.* To compound the difficulty, many of the terms have unfamiliar meanings, such as the earth's *crust.*

Text Features

Added to the demands of content and vocabulary are the special features of expository text—how expository text physically looks on the page. Unlike narrative text, which moves along from one event to the next without interruption other than an occasional chapter title or an illustration, expository text is frequently interrupted by headings and subheadings, pronunciations in parentheses, labels, footnotes, and a variety of graphics which must be carefully examined. Consider a typical nonfiction page.

A student faced with a page of expository text may be so overwhelmed by the physical presentation of the material that he or she doesn't know where to begin!

Text Structure

Another challenge to readers is the organizational structure of expository text. In contrast to narrative text, in which the plot flows from one event to the next, expository materials usually segment information into various topics.

The content is commonly structured in one of the following ways:

1. cause and effect,
2. compare and contrast,
3. problem and solution,
4. sequence or time order,
5. listing or description, or
6. a combination of the above.

In each new piece of expository text, the reader must uncover the organizational pattern in order to comprehend the relationship of ideas. Research has shown a strong link between a student's comprehension of expository text and his or her understanding of the way the text is organized (Seidenberg, 1989; Pearson and Fielding, 1991; Weaver and Kintsch, 1991).

Even if all these challenges make our heads swim, we must not forget the tremendous payoff that teaching our students to read nonfiction will have.

Why Is Nonfiction Important?

The ability to understand and write nonfiction is essential for school achievement (Seidenberg, 1989). Students will encounter a larger number of nonfiction texts as they progress through the grades, each posing special challenges. Students' success or failure in meeting these challenges has far-reaching consequences, as described in the following section.

Nonfiction Text and Standardized Tests: The Connection

With the passage of the *No Child Left Behind Act* in 2002, students are now required to take high-stakes, end-of-year tests to determine whether or not they can be promoted. These tests ask students to read both fiction and nonfiction, compare the two texts, and respond to them in writing. Teaching students to navigate and comprehend nonfiction texts throughout the year will help them succeed on these critical tests. The ongoing teaching of strategies useful for comprehending nonfiction texts in both reading and content area lessons is greatly preferred to the sudden and intense test prep practice in the weeks leading to the test that is so common in schools today. Students need time to practice and internalize these strategies. Frequent lessons and practice opportunities, such as those presented in this book, are ideal.

Increased World Knowledge

Teaching students to navigate and read nonfiction texts gives them access to a large body of important and useful information—information that they are not exposed to in everyday conversations but need in order to succeed in school, develop lifelong learning habits, pursue their interests, gain necessary skills, and become well-informed and responsible citizens. Plus, learning about the world around us is fascinating!

How Can We Prepare Students?

Research shows that understanding how text is organized helps readers construct meaning (Dickson, Simmons, and Kameenui, 1998). It follows that students need explicit instruction in text presentation and text structure as an aid to comprehending expository text. If students learn to read the signposts that are guides to the organization of a particular piece of nonfiction, they will be better equipped to make their way through the material.

One approach to teaching students how to read nonfiction—such as content area textbooks—is to build students' skills in identifying and using the various characteristics found in this type of text. For example:

* Learning to **preview** the title and headings in a chapter of social studies text will enable students to anticipate the main ideas that will be covered.

* Knowing how to use **text features**—graphic aids, such as diagrams, graphs, and time lines—will allow the reader to take additional meaning from them rather than viewing them as a disruption to the flow of the text. In addition, it will help students integrate this information with that provided by the text.

* Identifying the **text structure** will promote students' understanding and retention. Is the author comparing and contrasting life on the frontier with life in the cities? Is the text describing the physical characteristics of carnivorous dinosaurs?

Nonfiction surrounds us. The reasons for teaching our students efficient and effective strategies for tackling this type of text are compelling. What we must ask ourselves now is How?

How to Use This Book

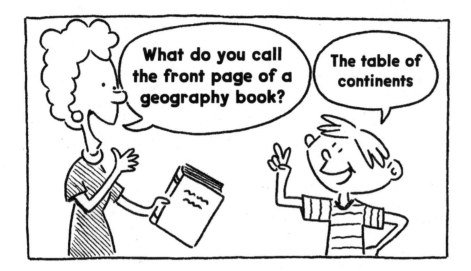

Teaching Students to Read Nonfiction provides 20 easy lessons that can be used during reading time or content area instructional time. The book includes:

- ❄ Easy-to-Use Text Feature Lessons
- ❄ Kid-Friendly Text Structure Lessons
- ❄ High-Interest Content Area Selections
- ❄ Assessment
- ❄ Purposeful Independent Practice
- ❄ Connections to Writing
- ❄ Web Sites and Graphic Organizers

What's in a Lesson?

There are two types of lessons in this book: Text Feature lessons and Text Structure lessons. **Text Feature lessons** focus on the typographical and visual elements commonly found in nonfiction. Or, to put it another way, how the text looks on the page. Students are guided through the process of using these visual tools with a portion of text. For ease of use, we have provided the text on a color transparency for each Text Feature lesson.

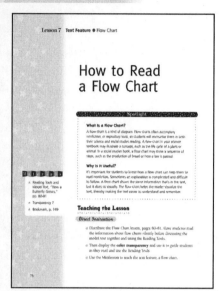

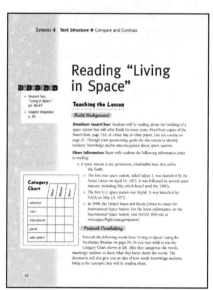

Text Feature lesson, see pages 78–79

Text Structure lesson, see pages 62–64

Students will encounter this same text feature as part of a longer selection in the following lesson, which focuses on text structures. The lessons are organized so that each Text Feature lesson is followed by a Text Structure lesson that includes the text feature of the previous lesson. The selections we have chosen are the type of nonfiction text that is typical of students' content area reading.

Text Structure lessons teach students how to recognize the organization of a piece of writing. The goal of repeated practice is to help students eventually identify text structures so they can use them more effectively to get information from their content area reading.

Learning About Text Features

Let's take a closer look at the organization of a **Text Feature lesson**. It focuses students' attention on how to navigate the text and how to identify and use "tools," such as headings and boldfaced words, that serve as an aid to comprehension. In addition, many students need advance preparation in how to read and interpret the graphic aids they are most likely to meet in nonfiction text—maps, charts, graphs, diagrams, and time lines. Therefore, the lesson also includes one type of graphic aid and teaches students how to read and interpret it. The Model Text for each Text Feature lesson is included on a color transparency. Later, in subsequent lessons, the same feature will be embedded in authentic text just as students would encounter it in their science and social studies textbooks. At this stage, students will practice reading text, stopping to refer to a graphic, and then returning to the text.

STUDENT MATERIALS

For each Text Feature lesson, students will receive a step-by-step guide called **Reading Tools**, on how to read the featured graphic aid. The accompanying **color transparency** of the graphic aid will facilitate group instruction and discussion.

The lessons covered in Teaching Students to Read Nonfiction help students read:

▲ *Diagrams*

▲ *Maps*

▲ *Flow Charts*

▲ *Time Lines*

▲ *Primary Sources*

▲ *Graphs*

▲ *Social Studies Textbooks*

▲ *Science Textbooks*

▲ *Encyclopedia Articles*

▲ *Online Sources*

▲ *Text with Multiple Features*

The Reading Tools are summarized on a **Bookmark** for later reference. These are provided on pages 148–150. Students can cut out each bookmark and save it in an envelope labeled **Reading Tool Kit**. Students will find these brief "memory joggers" helpful when they come upon the same graphic aid in their future content area reading.

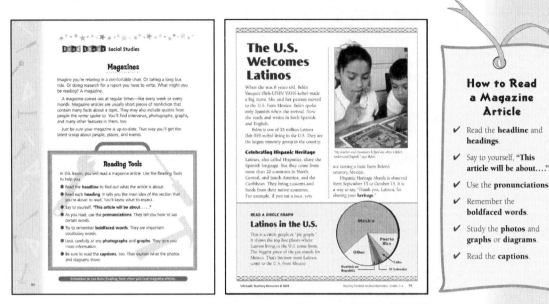

Reading Tools, Model Text, and Bookmark for a Text Feature lesson

Learning About Text Structures

Now let's focus on a **Text Structure lesson**. Informational texts have both a content and a structure. The structure is the organizational pattern within the text. (See the chart on page 14 for a list of the five major organizational patterns.) The structure ties the ideas together. Understanding both the content and the structure is essential for comprehension.

Things would be nice and simple if every piece of expository text were written in one identifiable pattern. However, informational text is complex, and an author may not use one text structure exclusively throughout a long piece of writing. More likely, only a section of text will be organized in a single pattern. For example, a science textbook chapter may:

※ first discuss different kinds of weather conditions (*description/listing*),

※ then go on to explain the patterns that result in particular kinds of weather (*cause and effect*),

※ follow up with a discussion of when a snowstorm officially becomes a blizzard or when a rainstorm is classified as a hurricane (*compare and contrast*), and finally

※ close with what to do in the event of severe weather, such as a tornado (*problem and solution*).

The 5 Most Common Structures of Nonfiction

Just like fiction, which has plot structure that students must learn and recognize, nonfiction follows basic structures, as well. Five kinds of text structures, or patterns of organization, are commonly found in informational texts:

1. **Description or listing** provides information, such as facts, characteristics, and attributes about a subject, event, person, or concept. This organization is the most common pattern found in textbooks (Niles, 1965; Bartlett, 1978). Here is an example:

   Polar bears eat plants, berries, fish, and meat. They can smell food from as far as 15 miles away.

2. **Sequence or time order** presents a series of events that take place in a time order. The author traces the sequence or the steps in the process. An example is:

   About five weeks later, the gills disappear, and the tadpole grows lungs.

3. **Compare and contrast** points out the likenesses and/or differences between two or more subjects. For example:

   The first astronauts ate food from tubes. The food was like baby food. Today, astronauts eat all kinds of food.

4. **Cause and effect** attempts to explain why something happens; how facts or events (causes) lead to other facts or events (effects). A single cause often has several effects. Also, a single event may have several causes. This paragraph describes causes and effects:

   Sound waves traveling through the ground make the bones in the snake's head vibrate. The bones send the signal to the snake's inner ear. That's how a snake hears.

5. **Problem and solution** describes a problem and presents one or more solutions to that problem. The following is an example:

   The Leaning Tower of Pisa was in danger of falling over. Engineers removed soil from one side of the tower to straighten it a little.

The long-term goal of text structure instruction is to enable students to recognize and use these structures flexibly so that they can make meaning from nonfiction texts.

SIGNAL WORDS

A good writer connects ideas within the text with words and phrases. These *connectives*, or *ties*, can act as signals to an informed reader who is trying to identify the text structure. The chart below shows some of the connectives that authors use to signal different text structures and the message they transmit to the reader.

Text Structures

Text Structure	👁 Signal Words	💡 Signal to Reader
Description or list	*such as, for example, for instance, most important, in front, beside, near*	A list or set of characteristics will follow.
Sequence or time order 1900 1950 2000 ①→②→③	*first, second, third, before, on (date), not long after, after that, next, at the same time, finally, then*	A sequence of events or steps in a process is being described.
Compare and contrast	*like, unlike, but, in contrast, on the other hand, however, both, also, too, as well as*	Likenesses and differences are being presented and/or discussed.
Cause and effect Problem and solution □→□	*therefore, so, this led to, as a result, because, if … then*	Evidence of cause(s) and effect(s) will be given or problems and solutions will be described.

This chart is Transparency 1

TEXT STRUCTURE LESSONS

We can see why readers must be explicitly taught to recognize and use text structures. Text structures are critical for constructing meaning, yet they are often difficult to identify for the developing reader. Therefore, in Text Structure lessons, two things happen:

1. **Students focus their attention on text structure.** They are taught what the text structures are and what clues they can use to identify the organization of a particular piece of writing. Students will get a minimum of two exposures to each of the text structures discussed above, plus many additional opportunities to apply what they have learned in their classroom content area reading. The repetition will give students the multiple exposures they need.

2. **The selection provides students with another opportunity to practice and apply the skills** that they were taught in the first part of the lesson. The same text features and graphic aids are embedded in informational text. A diagram, for example, might be part of a science article just as students would encounter it in their content area reading. Students will practice integrating information from the chart with the information in the text.

Using High-Interest Content Area Selections

As we have pointed out, the Model Texts provide students with an opportunity to apply the text feature that they have just learned about to a new text. These pieces have been carefully selected to match grade-level science and social studies standards. For example, in social studies, third graders will be reading about United States government; second graders will explore the wonders of plants and animals.

Some of the topics covered in this book include:

Science: animal life cycles, space, sound, and weather

Social Studies: American history, government, and communities

Assessment: Comprehension QuickCheck

Following the reading of each selection, the questions that are provided ask students to apply the skill in some or all of the following ways:

* identify the text feature

* use the text feature to get information

* generate other situations in which the text feature would be appropriate

Applying Through Purposeful Independent Practice

A true measure of students' knowledge is their ability to use a particular skill on their own. Not only do we teach students to use text features, but we also provide opportunities for them to practice getting information from these features in novel situations, and to create graphic features of their own such as charts, diagrams, and time lines to organize information learned from a text.

A **reproducible** is provided for each Text Structure lesson. The reproducible can be used either in class, in learning centers, or for homework. The purpose of this reproducible is to check students' comprehension of the text they read, using a graphic organizer to record new learning. These graphic aids, such as main idea charts, cause/effect charts, and Venn diagrams, are useful ways for students to organize the information in any text and serve as valuable models.

In addition, some of the **extension activities** at the bottom of the reproducibles ask students to organize new text using the text feature they learned about. For example, if students read about great inventions using a time line, they may be asked to create a time line to represent another time period, such as a year in their lives. Repeated opportunities to read and create these text features will help students organize their thinking when reading and writing independently. These features can be applied to written reports or oral presentations as well.

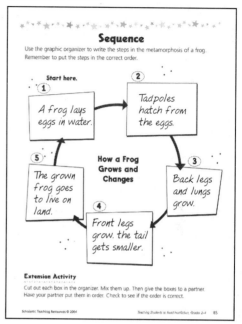

Possible answers:

Connecting to Writing

One of the ways to assess students' understanding of nonfiction text is by having them write brief **summaries**. Summarizing is an important reading strategy and critical writing skill. It involves selecting, organizing, and synthesizing the most important elements in a piece of text. By using their own words, students demonstrate what they have learned. Summaries include key ideas and details, are brief, do not contain the student's opinions, and are organized in a logical sequence. Summaries can be oral or written.

Summarizing is a very difficult skill for early readers. Laying the groundwork in the early grades is critical. You can do this by helping students identify main ideas in short texts such as paragraphs and assisting them as they write brief 3–4 sentence summaries of this text. Writing a good summary requires a great deal of modeling and guided practice (Hidi and Anderson, 1986).

In order to write a summary, a reader must be able to:

1 select the most important information in a text, thereby discarding the least important.

2. condense information by combining ideas or using a general term in place of a group of specific terms (i.e., "transportation" instead of "cars, trains, and planes").

3. record the most important ideas on paper in their own words.

To help students create a summary, follow these steps:

- ☀ Determine the main ideas, such as the main topic of the text. Use headings to help identify these main ideas.

- ☀ Look for information that is repeated. Be sure it is included only once in the summary. In addition, look for ideas that can be grouped.

- ☀ Look for the main idea sentence for each important section of text. It often appears in the heading or at the beginning of a paragraph.

- ☀ If you can't find a main idea sentence, think of one yourself.

- ☀ Write your summary. Be sure to use your own words and be brief (Cooper, 1993).

Tips for Choosing the Right Lesson

How you use the lessons in this book will depend on your classroom set-up and your preferences. You may follow the sequence presented in the book or, since each lesson can stand alone, you may choose to dip in wherever you see fit. Here are several options that will work:

- ☀ **In the self-contained classroom,** you may wish to approach each lesson as you would any reading skill—on a weekly or bi-weekly basis, following the sequence presented in this book. You can use the lessons to preteach text features and text structures, and later apply those skills to new text in social studies or science textbooks and periodicals. For example, you begin with the Overview Lesson that introduces the many features of nonfiction text using a magazine article as a model. At a later date when your students are reading other pieces of nonfiction such as a chapter in a social studies textbook, you can first review the features of nonfiction, including headings, photos, captions, and boldfaced words. Then students can apply what they learned to the new material in the text they are reading.

- ☀ **As an alternative, you can teach the lessons in this book during your social studies or science block.** Preview the science or social studies textbook lesson for the week and identify the text features and structures your students will encounter. Then preteach those skills using the appropriate lessons in this book. For example, if the science chapter includes a diagram showing the parts of a plant, you can preteach with Lesson 4—the text feature lesson on diagrams.

- ☀ **Another approach is to dip into just one part of a lesson.** You may teach a particular text feature, using the transparency, and leave the text structure lesson for another time. Or you may dip into the text structure part of the lesson, using only the longer selection.

Teaching the Lessons

Getting Started With Text Structure Lessons

▲▲▲▲▲▲▲▲▲▲▲▲▲▲▲▲▲▲▲▲▲▲▲▲▲▲▲▲

Throughout our teaching careers we have encountered many students who have struggled with nonfiction text: *What do I look at first? How can I get through this? What does all this mean?* These questions no longer go unanswered. Now we have powerful tools to help students not only navigate nonfiction text, but get them on the right path to comprehension. Text Feature lessons focus on the graphic elements of nonfiction, and each lesson highlights one feature. Text Structure lessons require more preparation: building students' background knowledge and preteaching vocabulary. This section provides helpful strategies for these important aspects of Text Structure lessons.

Building Background

Let's stop for a moment to talk about how you can prepare students *before* they begin reading the content area selection.

Prior knowledge is the background knowledge of the subject matter that a reader brings to a text; in other words, what a person already knows about the topic based on that person's experiences and beliefs.

Research (Cooper, 1993; Lapp, Flood, and Farnan, 1996) shows that activating prior knowledge before reading:

- ❋ helps the teacher assess the accuracy of what students already know.
- ❋ helps the teacher identify gaps in students' prior knowledge—information that students need to bring to the text in order to construct meaning.
- ❋ helps the learner construct meaning by making a connection between the new information and what is already known.
- ❋ helps the learner recall the new information after it is read.
- ❋ helps create motivation for learning.

Your role as teacher is to provide instructional scaffolds. Like the use of scaffolds in construction, you support, or lift up, students so that they can achieve what was not possible by themselves. As Vacca and Vacca (1999) state, "Instructional scaffolding allows teachers to support readers' efforts to make sense of texts while showing them how to use strategies that will, over time, lead to independent reading." So, while you are not preteaching the information students will read, you are filling in instructional gaps or dealing with misconceptions that would otherwise impede learning as they read.

For example, when we were teaching a lesson on the role of Congress, the text contained the following opening paragraph (*Congress*, Patricia Ryon Quiri, Children's Press, 1998):

In 1776, the United States declared its independence from Britain. Americans wanted to have their own government. They were tired of Britain telling them what to do. They knew they would have to fight long and hard to become independent. The Declaration of Independence signaled the beginning of the American Revolutionary War.

The rest of this excellent book details the Continental Congress, how the United States government was created, and how Congress works. But look at what you have to know to make sense of the opening paragraph. Our students needed to know:

- ❋ Britain is another name for England.
- ❋ In the 1700s, there was a group of people who came to settle this land from Britain, or England.
- ❋ The land belonged to England. It was not called the United States at that time.
- ❋ The settlers did not make their own laws. They had to obey the laws of England.
- ❋ Being independent meant having their own country. Then they could have their own government and make their own laws.
- ❋ In order to achieve independence, the settlers went to war with England.

Without this information, our students would have had difficulty grasping the historical context in which the Constitutional Convention created Congress. For example, some of our students weren't aware that the United States wasn't even a country at that time. Many were unaware of our country's connection to England. These and other informational gaps were impeding their understanding of the book.

SMART CHARTS

How can a teacher bridge the gap between what students know and what they need to know? One way is to use a **SmartChart** (Scholastic RED, 2002). The difference between a SmartChart and its classic cousin, the KWL chart, is the additional first column—Background. This column helps the teacher bring the students "up to speed" in terms of background information necessary to make meaning from the text. A SmartChart:

- ❋ prompts students to think about what they already know.

- ❋ provides an efficient way for you to tell students important background information that they need to know.

- ❋ encourages students to organize what they know, what they want to know, and what they learned from a reading selection.

- ❋ helps students set a purpose for reading.

- ❋ provides a place for students to review and record what they learned.

Sample SmartChart   **Selection: "Using Natural Resources"**

B Background	K What We Know	W What We Want to Know	L What We Learned
A natural resource is something found in nature that people can use. Water, air, trees, and soil are natural resources. People use natural resources for food, clothing, and shelter.	Trees can be used to make furniture and homes. Plants are grown in the soil for food.	What natural resources do we have in our community? How do we get natural resources? What natural resources are used to making clothing?	Water and air can be used to make electricity. People and animals need clean air to live. Wood is used to make paper. Oil is found deep in the ground. It is used for fuel for homes and cars.

There are many other techniques you can use, as well. You may also wish to share information before reading in the following ways:

- Show a picture that illustrates the concept or time period, or sets the scene.

- Read a section from a book that explains the necessary prior knowledge.

- List key facts on the chalkboard and discuss them with students.

When students use prereading tools (such as a SmartChart), prior knowledge is activated, helping them create a framework on which to hang new knowledge (Graves, Juel, and Graves, 1998).

To use a SmartChart, follow the four steps as modeled in the classroom snapshot below.

Setting: Mr. H. teaches second grade. His class is reading a selection about natural resources. He displays the chart and says: "Today we are going to read a book called How We Use the Earth. *This book is about our Earth's many natural resources and how we use them."*

1. Look for ways to build on and connect to student ideas when they share what they know. This is an ideal time to dispel misconceptions and correct inaccuracies. Student prior knowledge goes in the "What We Know" section. This is column head "**K**."

   Rosa: I know that we use trees for many things.

   Teacher: That's right. Trees are natural resources. What do we get or make from trees?

   John: We get fruit from trees.

   Komiko: We get wood from trees.

   Teacher: What do we use wood for?

2. Explain what students need to know so they can build "mental models," or pictures in their heads. This information goes in the background section. This is column head "**B**." You will fill this out with students as you present the information that they have not already shared but need to know.

   [*Teacher and students fill this out before reading.*]

3. Use the "What We Want to Know" column to help students set a purpose for reading and to build their curiosity. This is column head "**W**."

   Komiko: What else do we use wood for?

   Pablo: Is glass a natural resource?

Rosa: Is metal a natural resource?

John: I know we need air to breathe, but what is air used for?

4. Use the "What We Learned" column to review important concepts in the text. This is column head "**L.**"

> [*Teacher and students fill this out after reading as a summary of their learning. Students explain how and where they got the information.*]

Remember, the goal is to provide a support for students on which to hang the information they will read. You are not summarizing, preteaching, or outlining what they will read prior to reading. If the information is not in the text, but necessary to understand the text, it needs to be pretaught.

Preteaching Vocabulary

As you know from your own classroom experience, one of the many challenges facing students in their content area reading is vocabulary. Given the level of difficulty and the number of unfamiliar words that students are likely to encounter in a single chapter, you'll need to make several choices. One will be which words to teach. Another will be how to teach them.

Research shows that the direct teaching of vocabulary can help improve comprehension when we follow these guidelines (Cooper, 1993):

☀ **A few critical words are taught.** Limit the number of words to 3–5 and be sure that they are key to the main ideas in the text.

☀ **The words are taught in a meaningful context.** The context should reflect the particular meaning of the word in the text.

☀ **Students relate the new words to their background knowledge.** Students are more likely to remember words linked to other concepts and to words they already know.

☀ **Students are exposed to the words multiple times.** Students do not master new words after one presentation. Words have to be used in a variety of situations, including speaking and writing, before students "own" them.

SELECTING "JUST RIGHT" WORDS

There are a number of considerations you will want to take into account when deciding which words to teach directly (Cooper, 1993).

1. Begin by reviewing the text to identify the main ideas. The key concepts will serve as your basis for which words will require direct instruction and also as a guideline for activating prior knowledge.

2. Generate a list of words that are critical to understanding the main ideas that you've identified. These will be referred to as the "key-concept words."

3. Examine the text to see which key-concept words are defined or if their meanings are easily determined from context. Writers of expository text know that many of the words will be unfamiliar to students, so they include definitions within the text itself or context clues to help the reader determine the word's meaning. This is known as "considerate text." Below are three types of context clues. If the text contains such clues to a word's meaning, eliminate that word from your list because you will want to teach students to use these "unlocking the meaning" strategies during the reading of the text.

Types of Context Clues

Direct Definition: Direct definitions or explanations are the most obvious type of context clue. Words such as *is* and *means* signal that a definition or explanation of an unfamiliar word will follow.

> *One of the nicest things about living in Charleston is the* **climate**. *The climate* **is** *the kind of weather a place has over time.*

Restatement: Restatements are a type of context clue that uses different words to say the same thing. A restatement is often signaled by *or*, *that is*, and *in other words*, and is usually set off by commas.

> *Long ago, many African Americans* **migrated**, **or** *moved, from the South to the North to look for jobs.*

Compare and Contrast: Comparisons or contrasts are a kind of context clue that likens or contrasts an unfamiliar word or concept. Words and phrases, such as *like, just as, similar, different, in contrast,* and *on the other hand*, signal that a comparison or contrast of an unfamiliar word will follow.

> **Just as** *a drum* **vibrates** *when you hit it, a guitar string moves back and forth quickly when you pluck it to make sound.*

You'll want to keep track of these words on another list or highlight them on your copy of the text so you can take advantage of the "teachable moment" when students are reading. Students need these skills if they are to become independent at figuring out the meaning of unfamiliar words.

4. Some of the words on your list may contain structural elements that students can use to determine meaning. These words will not need to be taught directly. If they are stumbling blocks during reading, encourage students to use what they know about prefixes, suffixes, and root or base words to unlock meaning.

> explorer: er = one who
> reelect: re = again
> Triceratops: tri = three

5. Decide which words will probably be familiar to your students. These words may require only a quick review and not intensive instruction.

6. The words that remain on your list will require direct instruction. But if there are still too many, use your judgment to pare the list down to 3–5 words. You will not want to overwhelm students, so your final choice should be no more than 5 words.

The blood circulates through the body by flowing down one leg and up the other.

TEACHING THE WORDS

It is critical that students "own" the words we teach them. That is, students should be able to use the new words in speaking and writing. There are 4 levels of word knowledge (Dale and O'Rourke, 1971):

Level 1: "I never saw it before."

Level 2: "I've heard of it, but I don't know what it means."

Level 3: "I think it has something to do with . . ."

Level 4: "I know it."

The goal of word learning is Level 4.

VOCABULARY INSTRUCTIONAL ROUTINE

Here's an effective routine we have used with our students to introduce and teach new vocabulary. (Carnine et al, 1997)

Vocabulary Routine

Routine	Lesson Model
1. Use a visual, such as a picture/ photo in the text to be read.	**Teacher:** This is a statue of a pharaoh.
2. Model the pronunciation of the word.	Teacher writes the word **pharaoh** on the chalkboard. **Teacher:** This word is **FAIR-oh.** You say it.
3. Provide a synonym or a definition for each word. One way to define a word is to tell its class and then specify characteristics that make the word different from others in the same class.	**Teacher:** A **pharaoh** was a king in Egypt long ago. The rulers of other countries had different titles. In England, the title is king or queen. In China and Japan, the ruler was called an emperor or empress.
4. Check students' understanding.	**Teacher:** What is a pharaoh? **Student:** A pharaoh is what a king was called in Egypt a long time ago.
5. Give examples and non-examples. Students tell whether or not the example illustrates the definition of the word and explain why or why not.	**Teacher:** Was King Tut a pharaoh? **Student:** Yes, he was king of Egypt long ago. **Teacher:** Was Abraham Lincoln a pharaoh? **Student:** No. He was a president of the U.S. People voted for him.
6. Provide vocabulary activities so that students may review the words and their definitions.	Select from the activities on page 29. They include auditory sensitivity practice and cloze sentences.

Work With Words To review the words on subsequent days, place them in a larger context by connecting them to other words and concepts students know. This will deepen their understanding. Here are some effective strategies.

Vocabulary Teaching Strategies

Strategy	Purpose	When to Use	Comments
Concept or definition (word web)	Help students become independent word learners by teaching elements of a good definition	• Expository texts	Good support of strategy for independently inferring word meanings
Semantic mapping (web map)	Integrate prior knowledge and vocabulary learning	• Before or after reading • All texts	Develops in-depth word knowledge
Semantic feature analysis	Develop word knowledge by comparing words	• Before or after reading • Expository text and some narratives	Often more effective after reading
Hierarchical and linear arrays	Develop word relationships	• After reading • All texts	Encourages students to compare and contrast words
Preview in context	Use text context to develop word meanings	• Before reading • All texts	Must have text with good context clues
Contextual redefinition	Use context to determine word meaning	• Before reading • All texts	Useful when texts do not provide strong context clues
Vocabulary self-collection	Help students learn self-selected words	• After reading • All texts	Makes students responsible for own vocabulary learning

(Cooper, 1993)

Vocabulary Graphic Aids

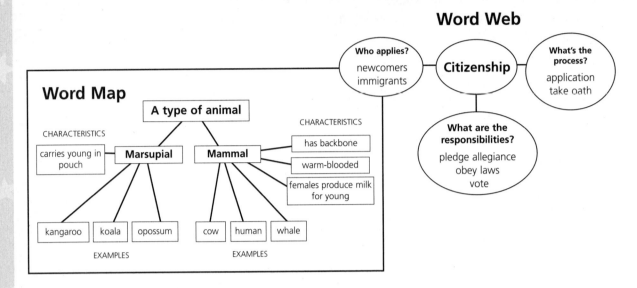

Word Web

Who applies?
newcomers
immigrants

Citizenship

What's the process?
application
take oath

What are the responsibilities?
pledge allegiance
obey laws
vote

Word Map

A type of animal

CHARACTERISTICS

carries young in pouch — **Marsupial**

Mammal — CHARACTERISTICS

has backbone

warm-blooded

females produce milk for young

kangaroo | koala | opossum

EXAMPLES

cow | human | whale

EXAMPLES

Semantic Feature Analysis

Fruit	Can Eat Skin/Peel	Grows on Trees	Round	Grows in Bunches
Apple	+	+	+	-
Orange	-	+	+	-
Banana	-	+	-	+
Grapes	+	-	+	+

Linear Array

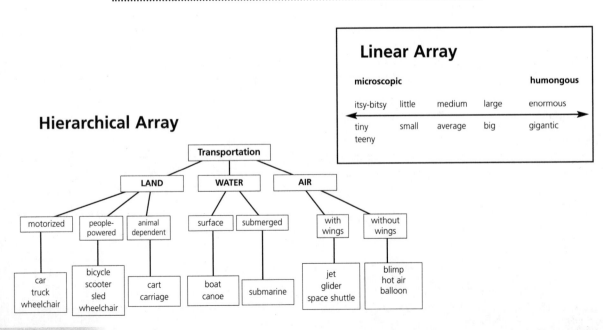

microscopic .... humongous

itsy-bitsy   little   medium   large   enormous

tiny   small   average   big   gigantic

teeny

Hierarchical Array

Transportation

LAND | **WATER** | **AIR**

motorized | people-powered | animal dependent | surface | submerged | with wings | without wings

car
truck
wheelchair

bicycle
scooter
sled
wheelchair

cart
carriage

boat
canoe

submarine

jet
glider
space shuttle

blimp
hot air
balloon

PROVIDE PRACTICE WITH VOCABULARY WORDS

The goal of all vocabulary instruction is to get students to be able to use the words in speaking and writing. Two useful activities include the following.

Oral Practice   Read aloud the sentences below. Have students listen for and identify the error in the sentence. It may be an incorrect pronunciation of the vocabulary word or another word. Ask students how the words are different: *What sound is different in each word?* Write the two words on the chalkboard and have students point out the spelling differences. Have students repeat the sentence using the correct word. For example:

1. We saw the adult butterfly emerge from its chrystalis. (*chrysalis*)

2. An anphibian can live equally well on land or in water. (*amphibian*)

3. Carnivals are animals that eat meat. (*carnivores*)

This practice improves students' auditory sensitivity and acuity in addition to reinforcing the vocabulary word.

Written Practice   Students can write cloze sentences for the vocabulary words. (Some students may find it easier to write a sentence that includes the targeted word and then rewrite the sentence using a blank for the word.) Have student partners exchange papers and complete the sentences.

1. A _____ is a cocoon. (*chrysalis*)

2. A turtle is an _____ because it lives on both land and in the water. (*amphibian*)

3. Herbivores only eat plants, whereas _____ eat meat. (*carnivores*)

ASSESS VOCABULARY WORDS

Have students react to open-ended statements about each vocabulary word. Their answers and explanations will allow you to quickly assess their understanding of the word (Beck, 1985). Write a "Yes or No?" statement on the board. Ask students to respond *yes* or *no* to each statement and give a short oral explanation for their answers. Explain that there are no right or wrong answers. Students will be giving their opinions.

Yes or No?

1. Carnivores are dangerous to people.   ___ yes___ no
2. A chrysalis is an amazing "shelter."   ___ yes___ no
3. An amphibian is like a fish.   ___ yes___ no

Here is an example of a teacher-student dialogue.

Teacher-Student Dialogue

Teacher: Read the first statement. What do you think—yes or no?

Student 1: I say no.

Teacher: Why?

Student 1: Because carnivores eat things like leaves, not people.

Teacher: (*Notes that student does not know the meaning of* carnivore. *Turns to the next student.*) Paul? Do you agree?

Student 2: I said no, but for a different reason. Even though carnivores are meat-eaters, most wouldn't harm people unless they were in the wild and felt threatened or were very hungry.

SUMMARY

The "Prepare to Read" portion of each lesson should take approximately 15 minutes. It is essential that key terms be defined and students' background knowledge activated before they begin the task of navigating a new piece of text.

So, you and your students are now ready to tackle nonfiction texts. In the following section, we provide a detailed, sample lesson carefully spread out over a week of instruction. This overview lesson is designed to help you introduce students to nonfiction text, and nonfiction text features and structures. It will also assist you as you establish classroom procedures for teaching nonfiction texts throughout the year.

Easy-to-Use Nonfiction Lessons

Overview Lesson

How to Read Nonfiction How many of you have ever taught a child to ride a bike? You may recall the eagerness of the child to just hop on and go, the frustration after the first few unsuccessful attempts, and finally the jubilation when the child realizes he CAN do it. Learning any new skill requires good instruction, lots of practice, and often a fair amount of time. When we teach our students a new skill, we give them opportunities to test out their use of the skill, a safe environment in which to make mistakes if they're not quite there, feedback and encouragement to help them correct their mistakes, and then time to revel in their learning when they know they have mastered the skill.

One Week, 30 Minutes a Day When it comes to learning about nonfiction, not only do our students need multiple teaching and practice opportunities, but they also need to get started on the right foot in order to understand what text structures and features are and why they're important. To help your class get started in the best possible way, we have provided a detailed Overview Lesson. In this lesson, we have carefully selected a nonfiction text that our students have enjoyed. Then, in just one week, 30 minutes a day, we will help you establish the routines and procedures you can follow all year to successfully teach your students how to navigate nonfiction text and learn from it. Here's a glimpse at what you'll do:

Stopping a Toppling Tower

Day 1: Introduce Nonfiction Text

You'll introduce your students to nonfiction text and find out what they know about this important text type. Engaging your students in a conversation about great nonfiction books they've read, topics they're interested in reading about, and nonfiction books you like and recommend is a great way to motivate students and set up a classroom environment in which nonfiction is read, discussed, learned from, and enjoyed.

Day 2: Prepare to Read

You'll introduce your students to a nonfiction article called "Stopping a Toppling Tower." You will build background and preteach vocabulary using the teaching routines provided. Since these will be used all year, it's beneficial to take the time to discuss in depth each aspect of each routine to help you and your students become familiar with the routine.

Day 3: Teach Text Features and Read the Selection

You'll read with students the nonfiction article, "Stopping a Toppling Tower," focusing on the text features. As you guide students in the reading, you will be reinforcing the Reading Tools that students have learned for navigating nonfiction text.

Day 4: Teach Text Structure and Reread the Selection

You'll revisit the text to focus on its text structure—problem and solution. Since identifying text structure is difficult, it is best to address text structure *after* students have had the opportunity to read and work through any comprehension difficulties in the text. A second reading will allow students to focus on more sophisticated aspects of the text since comprehension difficulties will have been addressed in the first reading.

Day 5: Check Comprehension and Apply to Writing

After two readings of the text, you will now take the opportunity to check students' comprehension *and* their ability to apply their learning to new texts.

As the year progresses, students will become more adept at identifying and learning from text structures and features. Remind students that this is hard work, takes time, and is worth the effort. The goal in the primary grades is to expose students to nonfiction text so that they are as comfortable with it as they are with fiction. Soon, reading nonfiction texts will not only be easier, but it will be fun, too!

"Stopping a Toppling Tower"

Day 1: Introduce Nonfiction Text

What's Special About Nonfiction?

Explain to students that they will be reading a great deal of nonfiction not only throughout this year, but also every year as they move up through the grades. Point out that students already read nonfiction because it surrounds us. Every time they read about a favorite animal, a famous person, or even the lunch menu, they are reading nonfiction.

Nonfiction gives information. It explains, informs, or persuades. Explain that nonfiction materials are quite different from a story or a novel, and that reading nonfiction often presents more challenges than reading fiction. Make students aware of some of the reasons for this by discussing the following characteristics of nonfiction. Demonstrate by showing examples from a chapter in your social studies or science textbook.

Characteristics of Nonfiction Text

1. Nonfiction looks different from fiction.
   - In addition to a chapter title, there are usually headings throughout the text.
   - There is often a variety of fonts and type sizes on each page.
   - Words in a paragraph may be boldfaced or italicized.
   - Diacritical markings may follow some words to show pronunciations.

2. Graphic aids such as diagrams, maps, charts, and photographs are usually included. They explain the information in the text or give additional information and must be examined carefully with attention to captions and labels.

3. The topic probably contains unfamiliar vocabulary. There are often multisyllabic words, such as *photosynthesis*, that may be difficult to pronounce.

4. There is a great deal of information to be understood and remembered.

Materials

▲ Reading Tools and Model Text, "Stopping a Toppling Tower," pp. 40–42

▲ Transparencies 2–3

▲ Graphic Organizer, p. 47

▲ Bookmark, p. 148

Tell students that the good news is they can learn how to navigate their way through the challenges of reading nonfiction. And although they may find it hard to believe, many of the features that make nonfiction seem daunting actually are "clues" to help them understand what they're reading. Reassure students that they can learn how to identify these clues and use them to read more skillfully. And it doesn't take a Sherlock Holmes!

Share Experiences With Nonfiction

Ask students to share experiences they've had with nonfiction. Questions such as these may get the ball rolling: *What books about real people, places, and events have you read in the last couple of months? Do you enjoy reading these types of books? Why or why not? When you read an article or a biography, do you look at the illustrations and read the captions, or do you skip them?*

Show students your copy of *Teaching Students to Read Nonfiction* and explain how it will help them (see Think Aloud at left).

The lesson that follows provides students with an overview of a representative piece of nonfiction text. It is a magazine article that contains many of the features common to all nonfiction text. The purpose of this lesson is to make students aware of these features. The reading strategies presented will help prepare them for reading materials as diverse as their social studies textbook, an online encyclopedia entry, or a social studies feature in a periodical.

Day 2: Prepare to Read

Build Background with a SmartChart

Tell students that they will read an article about the Leaning Tower of Pisa. Distribute copies of the **SmartChart**, page 152, or create one on chart paper.

❋ Ask students what they know about the Leaning Tower of Pisa. Their statements will inform you of any gaps or misconceptions in their prior knowledge. As students share information, record it in column 2, What We **K**now, of the SmartChart. Through your questioning, guide the discussion so that students share what they know about where the tower is located, why it is so famous, and what the problem is with the tower. General facts about other buildings, though they may be interesting, will not be helpful background for comprehending the article.

❋ Based on what you learned about the gaps or misconceptions in your students' prior knowledge, share with them the background knowledge they will need to comprehend "Stopping a Toppling Tower." Record the background information you discussed in column 1 of the chart, **B**ackground.

- The Leaning Tower of Pisa is located in the city of Pisa in Italy. It is one of Italy's most famous structures; thousands of tourists visit it every year and climb to the top.

- The tower has always tilted. Building began 900 years ago in 1173. When the structure was three stories high, it started to lean. When architects tried to correct the problem, the building began to tilt the other way! Despite the tilt, work on the tower continued until it was topped off with a bell tower in 1350.

- In the last 300 years, the tilt has gotten worse. It has increased about $\frac{1}{20}$ of an inch every year. There was fear that eventually the tower would fall.

- Finally, in 1990, the tower had to be closed to visitors.

❋ Finally ask students if the discussion raised questions that they would like to find the answers to. List these under What We **W**ant to Know.

❋ Have students complete the chart after they read the article.

Preteach the following words from "Stopping a Toppling Tower" using the Vocabulary Routine on page 26. Or you may wish to use the Knowledge Rating Chart shown on the next page.

As you read, help students define *cable, topple,* and *compression* by using the context clues in the text.

Define each word and provide an example sentence. Also point out any unusual pronunciations, synonyms, antonyms, and related words.

✶ **tilt** To lean to one side. *If I tilt my chair back, it may fall.*
Synonyms for *tilt* are *lean* and *slant.*
Point out the related word *tilted,* and its antonym, *straight.*

✶ **engineers** People who plan, design, and build or repair roads, bridges, buildings, and machinery. *The engineers designed the building to be safe if there was an earthquake.*
Help students pronounce the word correctly.
Students will most likely know an engineer as a driver of a train or locomotive. Discuss the fact that this is a word with multiple meanings and stress the meaning that is used in this selection.

✶ **landmark** A familiar building or object that stands out, so that people can use it to find their way. *The hikers knew they were walking in the right direction, because they saw a familiar landmark— the City Hall tower—in the distance.*

✶ **foundation** The base or lowest part of a building that supports everything above it. *A tall building needs a strong and deep foundation to support it.*

Have each student rate his or her knowledge of the vocabulary words. Follow up with a discussion of which words are the easiest, the most difficult, and the most unfamiliar to the greatest number of students. Encourage students to share what they know about the words. The discussion will also give you an idea of how much knowledge students bring to the concepts they will be reading about.

Knowledge Rating Chart
How Much Do You Know About These Words?

	I know what it means	I've heard it, but I'm not sure what it means.	I've never seen it or heard it.
tilt			
engineers			
landmark			
foundation			

Day 3: Teach Text Features and Read the Selection

Direct Instruction

STEP 1

Distribute the student lesson, pages 40–42, and display the **color transparency** of "Stopping a Toppling Tower."

STEP 2

Guide students through the student section **How to Read Nonfiction**.

- ❉ Have students comment on what they see are the differences between a page in a story and the page displayed on the transparency.

- ❉ Explain that the **Reading Tools** will help them figure out how to use the features on a page of nonfiction. Point out that each tool highlights one of the features in the text and explains how it helps the reader.

STEP 3

Walk students through the **Reading Tools**. As students read each item, have them identify the corresponding feature and callout on the transparency.

- ❉ Point out that photographs, diagrams, and charts are examples of **graphic aids**. Graphic aids illustrate information; they help the reader visualize what's in the text. Some graphic aids also add important information.

- ❉ In this article, the **photograph** helps the reader visualize the subject—the Leaning Tower of Pisa.

- ❉ The **diagram** also helps students visualize what they read by illustrating the type of soil that was discussed in the article.

STEP 4

Have students read the model text, "Stopping a Toppling Tower," silently before discussing it together. Remind them to look for special **text features**—headings, boldfaced words, pronunciations—and use each one to help them better understand what they are reading.

STEP 5

Use the Minilesson to model how you approach a page of nonfiction.

Preview Routine

An activity that will be extremely helpful to students before they begin to read a selection is previewing the text. A preview informs students about the content of the material and gives them a framework for reading. Use the following procedure to demonstrate the usefulness of previewing the text. You may wish to distribute the Prereading Organizer reproducible on page 154. Use as needed to help students learn the preview routine.

* First, have students read the title of the selection and browse the photos or illustrations. If headings and subheadings exist, point them out and explain how they relate to the selection's main ideas. Write the title (and headings) on the chalkboard. Ask students what they think the text will be about.

* Then, ask students what they expect to learn from the selection. Record their answers.

* After students complete the reading, ask them to tell in two or three sentences what the text was about. Suggest that students use the title, headings, and subheadings to guide them. Compare what they say to their original prediction.

Nonfiction Text

When you read **nonfiction**, you learn information. Science and social studies articles are one kind of nonfiction. They give you information about a topic like wolves or great explorers.

Take a look at the nonfiction article on pages 41–42. You can see that it looks very different from a storybook. How? You see a title, headings, and numbers—all in different sizes. There are also special features, such as the photograph, diagram, and box at the bottom of the page. And instead of reading across the page from left to right, you have to read two columns.

All of this stuff may be very confusing. However, each feature is a tool, just like a hammer or a can opener. A tool helps you do your work. Nonfiction tools help you understand what you are reading. But first you have to learn how to use them.

Reading Tools

Use the tools below to help you read "Stopping a Toppling Tower."

◉ Read the **title**. It tells you the big topic, or what the article is about.

◉ Read the **introduction** and the **headings**. They are clues about the main ideas in the article.

◉ As you read the article, try to remember the words in **boldfaced type**. They are important vocabulary words.

◉ A **pronunciation** after a word tells you how to say the word.

◉ Read the text **in order**. Read the list that says *The Problem* first. Then go on to the list that says *The Solution*.

◉ Study the **photograph** and the **diagram**. They give you more information.

Remember to use these Reading Tools when you read any nonfiction.

Stopping A Toppling Tower

by Mary Kay Carson

Every year, the Leaning Tower of Pisa (PEA-zuh) tilts a fraction of an inch farther! If it tilts too far, this famous Italian building could topple or crash to the ground. Scientists had to find a way to save the tower—without making it a "Straight Tower of Pisa."

It's amazing but true that the tower has been tilted ever since it was built more than 900 years ago. The problem is that each year it leans a tiny bit more. In 1990 **engineers** said that the tower was in danger of toppling. The building was no longer safe. It had to be closed to visitors.

For years, engineers and scientists had been thinking about how to stop the tower from falling over. After considering many ideas, they agreed on a possible solution. In 1998, engineers started work to save the **landmark**.

The Problem

1. The tower weighs 14,000 tons. Wind pushes from the sides. Sometimes there are small earthquakes that rattle the building. These forces weaken the slanted tower.

2. Tall, skinny shapes are hard to balance. A skinny tower has a small **foundation**. That makes it easy for it to tilt too far to one side. Then—TIMBER!

3. The tower is built on soft sand and clay. The heavy building squishes the soft soil beneath it. That makes the tower slowly sink. Why does it lean? The soil is softest under the tower's low side, so that side sinks more.

4. As the tower leans, more of its weight rests on the lower side. That **compression**, or squeezing, could cause the tower to tip over.

The Solution

1. First, workers wrapped steel **cables** around the tower. The cables were heavy ropes made of steel wire. Workers hooked the ends of the cables to heavy weights. If the tower started to topple, the cables would hold it up.

2. The workers started to dig under the high side of the tower (the right side in the photo). They slowly and carefully took away some of the soil. They hoped that the tower would sink a little on that side. It did—by one inch! That may not sound like much, but it was enough to make the tower straighter.

3. No one can <u>see</u> the change in the tilt of the tower, but now it's safe. It was reopened in January 2002. Once again, visitors come from all over the world to see it and climb to the top. Engineers expect that the tower will stand— tilted—for centuries to come.

Thanks, But No Thanks...

People have sent hundreds of tower-fixing ideas to the Italian government. Why do you think these four ideas were rejected? What ideas do you have?

1. Freeze the ground under the tower.
2. Slice off the top to make the tower lighter.
3. Hitch a car to the tower and pull the tower straight.
4. Stuff rice and beans under the low side. When the foods absorb water, they will swell and push up the tower.

below ground level

sandy mud layer

clay layer

Day 4: Teach Text Structure and Reread the Selection

What Do My Students Need to Know About Text Structures?

Just as we teach story structure and story mapping when students read fiction, we also need to introduce students to the structure of nonfiction. In the lower grades, we want to build an awareness of what text structure is. Our goal is not to hold students responsible for identifying the internal organization of nonfiction text. Rather, we are laying the groundwork for their understanding of this complicated but extremely important skill, so that they can use it in the upper grades where nonfiction dominates their reading.

Text structures are more difficult to identify and use than text features. Therefore, when introducing text structure it is best to work with a text students have already read. Their familiarity with the content will enable students to focus on more sophisticated aspects of the text's organization. You may think that you're being repetitive, but your students will need to hear again and again (1) what text structures are and (2) what clues they can use to identify the text structure of a piece of writing. Remember, our aim is exposure. And if some students achieve some degree of mastery, so much the better!

Five Text Structures

Students are most likely to meet five text structures in their textbooks and other nonfiction materials. As you discuss them, display **Transparency 1**.

- **Description** The writer gives information about a topic, a person, or an animal. An example of this is an article that describes elephants, tells where they are found, and gives an account of the groups in which they live.

- **Sequence** The author tells about events that happen in a time order, such as events in the life of Martin Luther King, Jr., or describes the steps in a process, such as how bread is made.

- **Compare and Contrast** The writer points out what's the same and what's different between two subjects. A science article about alligators and crocodiles is an example.

- **Cause and Effect** The writer explains why something happens. A news report about what happens during a hurricane would discuss cause and effect.

- **Problem and Solution** The author describes a problem and tells what was done to solve it, as in an article about beached whales and what people did to save them.

Why Are They Helpful?

Students may wonder why it is important to identify text structure in nonfiction. They need to know that a reader who is aware of the pattern that is being used can anticipate the kind of information that will be presented. If we know that a text is organized around compare and contrast, we expect to read about the likenesses and differences between people or events. This gives us a framework for connecting the ideas and remembering them. And, of course, this makes us more skillful readers and thinkers.

How Can Text Structure Be Identified?

The text structure of the article "Stopping a Toppling Tower" is **problem and solution**. How does the reader know? The author tells the reader. The first paragraph of the article states that there is a "problem." The second paragraph states that engineers have found a "solution."

Headings are also clues. The headings **The Problem** and **The Solution** clearly tell the reader what will follow. It's important for students to become aware of possible clues in the text and begin to look for them as they read.

Have students reread "Stopping a Toppling Tower," this time focusing on the text structure that the author has used to present the information. Use the Minilesson to introduce the concept of text structure.

Think Aloud

When I read that this article was about a tower that could topple, I said to myself, "That's a problem!" Then, in the paragraph after the introduction, the writer uses the word problem. *In the next paragraph, I read the word* solution. *There are two numbered lists that are headed "The Problem" and "The Solution." All these signals tell me that this article will explain a problem and tell how it was solved. Now I know what to look for when I read—and what to remember, too.*

Teaching the Text Structure:
Problem and Solution

▲▲▲▲▲▲▲▲▲▲▲▲▲▲▲▲▲▲▲▲▲▲▲▲▲▲▲▲▲▲▲▲▲▲▲▲▲

Introduce Explain to students that a writer of nonfiction organizes information in ways called text structures. Knowing how the writing is organized helps the reader understand and remember what he or she reads.

The information that students read in their science and social studies textbooks and in magazine articles is most often structured in one of five ways:

- **Compare and Contrast** The writer points out what's the same and what's different between two things, such as frogs and toads.

- **Description** The writer gives information about a person, a place, or an animal.

- **Sequence** The writer tells about events that happen in a time order, such as events in the life of Harriet Tubman. Or the writer describes the steps in a process, such as how sneakers are made.

- **Problem and Solution** The author describes a problem and tells what was done to solve it, such as how an endangered animal was saved.

- **Cause and Effect** The writer explains why something happens, such as why rain turns to snow.

Possible answers:

Discuss the importance of identifying how text is structured. It alerts the reader to how the text was written. This knowledge can help readers organize their thinking as they read. For example, the reader thinks, "The writer is going to compare and contrast. That means I'll be reading about how things are the same and how they are different. I'll look for those likenesses and differences as I read."

Model Use the Think Aloud on page 44 to model how you figured out that the text structure of "Stopping a Toppling Tower" is problem and solution.

Guided Practice/Apply Have students read the article. Distribute copies of the graphic organizer for problem and solution, page 47. Ask students to fill it out as they read. You may wish to have students work individually or as a group.

Day 5: Check Comprehension and Apply to Writing

Comprehension QuickCheck

After you have completed the lesson, you may use the following questions to check students' comprehension:

1. Why is the Leaning Tower of Pisa so famous? (*It's the only building in the world that leans so much.*)

2. What was the problem with the tower? (*Every year, it leaned a tiny bit more. It was in danger of toppling.*)

3. How did engineers solve the problem? (*Answers should reflect an understanding of the steps taken.*)

4. Which text features did you find most helpful? (*Answers will vary.*)

5. What clues in the article helped you figure out the text structure? (*Answers should reflect the signals that the writer of the article provided the reader.*)

Independent Practice: Writing

Have students write two or three sentences that tell about the article. Ask them to include the following:

* ✳ what happened to make the Leaning Tower of Pisa dangerous,

* ✳ what was done to make the tower safe again.

Problem and Solution

Write the problem and solution in "Stopping a Toppling Tower."

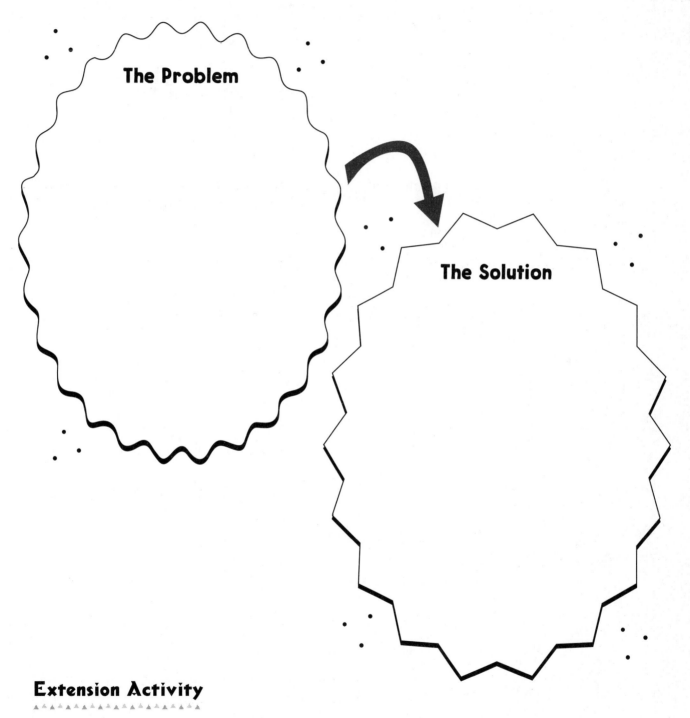

The Problem

The Solution

Extension Activity

Write two news reports about the Leaning Tower of Pisa. Date the first one November 1990. Date the second one January 2002. Draw a picture for each news report.

How to Read an Encyclopedia Article

Spotlight

What Is an Encyclopedia?

An encyclopedia contains nonfiction articles about many topics. The topics are arranged in alphabetical order. An encyclopedia can be in print or online. Online/Internet encyclopedias offer the advantage of additional features such as web links and clickable photos.

Why Is It Useful?

An encyclopedia is a great way to find concise, expert information on a topic. Online encyclopedias offer the advantage of quick, up-to-date information. In addition, they are easy to access and can be used at home, at school, in the library, or anywhere else a computer exists. Therefore, they save a lot of time and expense.

Materials

▲ Reading Tools and Model Text, "Penguin," pp. 50–51

▲ Transparency 4

▲ Bookmark, p. 148

Teaching the Lesson

Direct Instruction

✹ Distribute the Encyclopedia lesson, pages 50–51. Have students read the information about encyclopedias silently before discussing the model text together and using the Reading Tools.

✹ Then, use the **color transparency** to guide students as they read and use the Reading Tools.

✹ Use the Minilesson on page 49 to teach the text feature.

Teaching the Text Feature

Introduce Encyclopedias Point out that an encyclopedia contains nonfiction articles about many topics. An encyclopedia can be in print or online. Online encyclopedias contain web links for additional, related information. Tell students they should do the following to read an encyclopedia article:

- Read the **title** to learn what the article is about.
- Scan for **headings** to identify main ideas in the text. They also tell readers about the topic of upcoming sections.
- Look for other text features such as **photographs, charts, maps, and underlined topics** that can provide more information. Readers can click on links in an online encyclopedia to get more information.

Model Use the Think Aloud at right to model how to read an encyclopedia article.

Guided Practice/Apply Have students read "Penguin" on page 51 to learn about this interesting animal. Make sure they can navigate the encyclopedia article and understand its unique features. Ask them to retell the information in their own words. You may also wish to ask the following:

1. How are penguins different from other birds? (*They cannot fly. They have flippers instead of wings. Tiny feathers cover their entire bodies. They spend most of their time in water.*)
2. How do penguins move on land? (*They waddle slowly as they walk.*)
3. What is the most interesting thing you learned about penguins? (*Answers will vary, but should be supported.*)
4. Where else could you find information about penguins? (*other encyclopedias, online articles, books about animals, and so on*)

Think Aloud

The title tells me that this encyclopedia entry is about penguins. I see that the article is divided into three sections—the introduction, information on how penguins move on land, and information on how penguins are alike and different from other birds. The section headings are the main ideas in the article.

I also see a photograph. This helps me see what penguins really look like. I can compare what I read to the photograph.

Comprehension QuickCheck

You may use the following questions to check students' comprehension:

1. What is an encyclopedia? (*a collection of nonfiction articles about a host of topics*)
2. Why is an encyclopedia helpful? (*You can find information quickly and easily.*)
3. What special features does this encyclopedia article contain? (*photographs*)
4. If you wanted to learn about another animal, which would you choose— an encyclopedia or a book on animals? Why? (*Answers will vary, but should be supported.*)

Encyclopedia Article

Suppose you wanted to learn more about an animal. Where does the animal live? What does it eat? What does it look like? You can use an **encyclopedia** to find these and other facts. An encyclopedia contains nonfiction articles about many topics.

Reading Tools

In this lesson, you will be reading an encyclopedia article. Use the Reading Tools below to help you read an encyclopedia entry.

- First, **preview** the article.

- Begin by reading the **title** of the article. It tells you what the article is about.

- Next, find the **headings**. They divide the article into parts. Each heading tells you the main idea of the part.

- Finally, look at the **pictures**. They give you more information and help you understand the article.

Remember to use these Reading Tools when you read an encyclopedia article.

Penguin

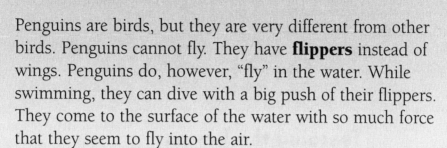

Penguins are birds, but they are very different from other birds. Penguins cannot fly. They have **flippers** instead of wings. Penguins do, however, "fly" in the water. While swimming, they can dive with a big push of their flippers. They come to the surface of the water with so much force that they seem to fly into the air.

How Penguins Move on Land

Penguins stand up straight like a person on land. They waddle slowly along when they walk, and use their flippers for balance.

When they walk over snow and ice, penguins may flop on their bellies. In this position, they "row" with their feet. They also use their flippers when they are in a great hurry. This way of traveling is called **tobogganing**.

Penguins and Other Birds

Unlike other birds, the feathers of a penguin cover its entire body. The feathers are very tiny and close together. They keep the penguin warm and dry. Unlike most birds, penguins spend most of their lives in water. They are very **social** birds. They live with thousands of other penguins.

Reading "Polar Bear"

M a t e r i a l s

▲ Student Text, "Polar Bear," pp. 56–57

▲ Graphic Organizer p. 55

Teaching the Lesson

Build Background

Distribute SmartChart Students will be reading an encyclopedia article about polar bears, an animal found in the Arctic. Distribute copies of the SmartChart, page 152, or create one on chart paper. Use the routine on page 21. Through your questioning, guide the discussion to identify students' knowledge and/or misconceptions about polar bears.

Share Information Share with students the following information prior to reading, as needed:

✲ Polar bears live on the northern coast of Alaska, Canada, Greenland, Russia, and on the islands in the Arctic Ocean.

✲ Polar bears can smell food 10–15 miles away.

✲ Polar bears can live in severe cold (-40 or -50 degrees Fahrenheit) because of their thick layer of blubber (4.5 inches) and two layers of fur.

Preteach Vocabulary

Preteach the following words from "Polar Bear" using the Vocabulary Routine on page 26. Or you may wish to use the Knowledge Rating chart shown at left. After each student rates his or her knowledge of the words, follow up with a discussion of which words are the easiest, most difficult, and most unfamiliar to the greatest number of students. Encourage students to share what they know about the words. The discussion will also give you an idea of how much knowledge students bring to the concepts they will be reading about.

Knowledge Rating Chart

	Can Define	Know Some Information About	Don't Know
climate			
fur			
icy			
male			
paws			

As you read, help students define the word *tracks* by using the context clues in the text.

Define each word. Be sure to point out unusual pronunciations, related words, and other aspects of the word.

- ❊ **climate** The usual weather in a place.
  Focus on the pronunciation of the word.

- ❊ **fur** Soft, thick, hairy coat of an animal.
  Focus on the related word *hair*.

- ❊ **icy** Very cold, or covered with ice.
  Focus on the related words: *ice, icicle, ice-skate, icing.*

- ❊ **male** A person or animal that can father young.
  Focus on related words: *boy, man, dad, father.*
  Introduce the opposite: *female.*

- ❊ **paws** The foot of an animal having four feet and claws.
  Focus on the related word: *foot.*

Read the Selection

- ❊ Distribute copies of "Polar Bear," pages 56–57. Have students preview the selection using the Preview Routine on page 39. Then, guide students as they apply the strategies they have learned for navigating text. Remind students to use the Reading Tools to read the article provided.

- ❊ Before the second reading, use the lesson below to teach students about the selection's text structure: description.

Teaching the Text Structure: Description

Introduce Discuss with students the importance of identifying how text is structured. It alerts readers to how the text was written. This can help readers organize their thinking as they read. Tell students that a science article often provides details about a topic.

Model You may wish to use the Think Aloud at right as you model how to determine the text structure of "Polar Bear."

Guided Practice/Apply As students reread the selection, have them complete the fact chart, page 55. Then have students work in pairs to retell the information in their own words.

Think Aloud

Writers organize their writing in a way that helps us understand it. As I look at "Polar Bear," I see a lot of details. For example, I see facts about where polar bears live, what they eat, and how they look. The author has provided a description of this interesting, Arctic animal. As I read on, I will remember these details.

After you have completed the lesson, you may use the following questions to check students' comprehension:

1. Where do polar bears live? (*in the cold Arctic*)

2. What do polar bears eat? (*plants, berries, fish, and meat*)

3. Why don't a polar bear's claws show up in its tracks? (*Their fur and padded paws keep them above the snow.*)

4. How did the photographs add to your understanding of polar bears? (*Answers will vary.*)

5. What else would you like to learn about polar bears? How would you find this information? (*Answers will vary.*)

Independent Practice: Writing

Have students write a summary of the information they just read. Suggest that they use the chart they completed while reading to help them create their summaries. Have them include the following:

* what polar bears look like,
* where polar bears live,
* what polar bears eat.

Possible answers:

WebLinks

www.antarcticaconnection.com/	Antarctica Connection
www.polarbearsalive.org	Polar Bear International
www.seaworld.org/infobooks/PolarBears/home.html	
	Sea World
www.nwf.org	National Wildlife Federation
www.sandiegozoo.org	San Diego Zoo
kidscience.minigco.com	Science/Nature for Kids
www.inhs.uiuc.edu/chf/pub/virtualbird/educational.html	
	For the Birds

Polar Bears

Use the graphic organizer below to record facts about polar bears.

What Polar Bears Look Like

What Polar Bears Eat

Why Polar Bears Make Tracks Without Claws

Extension Activity

Write an encyclopedia entry for another animal you think others would like to know about.

POLAR BEAR

Polar bears can live very well in the cold Arctic climate. This is because they have a thick layer of fat under their fur. It keeps them warm. It also helps them float in the icy water. Polar bears travel very far to find food. Then they make a "bed" in the snow to sleep.

Polar bears are big! Some males can be as tall as 10 feet (3 meters). They can be more than 800 pounds (360 kilograms). Polar bears use their front paws to swim. Their paws can be one foot (30 centimeters) across.

FOOD

Polar bears eat plants, berries, fish, and meat. They can smell food from as far as 15 miles (24 kilometers) away.

Polar bears can carry more than 200 pounds (90 kilograms) of food in their bellies. Their bellies stretch to hold all this! They need to eat big meals because sometimes they can't catch food.

TRACKS

Polar bears make tracks in the snow. Their claws don't show up in these tracks. This is because their fur and padded paws keep their claws above the snow.

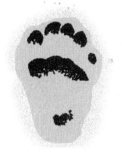

How to Read a Diagram

M a t e r i a l s

▲ Reading Tools and Model Text, "Space Suits," pp. 60–61

▲ Transparency 5

▲ Bookmark, p. 148

Spotlight

What Are Diagrams?

A diagram is a special picture that shows the parts of something or how something works. Some diagrams contain numbers or letters to show how to read the information. Others contain arrows to direct the reader. Diagrams help to clarify or illustrate difficult information for a reader.

Why Are They Useful?

Diagrams show a lot of information in a limited space. Diagrams also help to make information clear for a reader. For example, a diagram can illustrate a complex process such as the water cycle or photosynthesis. Without understanding all of the complicated details involved in the process, a reader can get a general sense of the process from the diagram. The text accompanying the diagram provides the details. Also, visualizing information can help a reader remember it. Therefore, diagrams are great visual aids to study and learn from.

Teaching the Lesson

Direct Instruction

❋ Distribute the Diagram lesson, pages 60–61. Have students read the information about diagrams silently before discussing the model text together and using the Reading Tools.

❋ Then, use the **color transparency** to guide students as they read and use the Reading Tools.

❋ Use the Minilesson on page 59 to teach the text feature.

Teaching the Text Feature

Introduce Diagrams Point out that diagrams are special pictures that show the parts of something or how something works. To read a diagram students should do the following:

- First, read the **title** and **introduction**. They tell readers what the diagram is about. Look at the whole page. Notice how the information is presented.
- Look at the **labels**. These are important words to remember. They tell readers the important parts of the diagram. Read them to learn more about the picture.
- Follow the **arrows**. The arrows connect the labels to the picture.
- Finally, look for **pronunciations**. They are sometimes provided and help readers say new or difficult words.

Model Use the Think Aloud at right to model how to read diagrams.

Guided Practice/Apply Have students read "Space Suits" on page 61 to learn about the clothing worn in outer space. Make sure they can navigate the article and understand a diagram's unique features. Ask them to retell the information in their own words. You may also wish to ask the following:

1. What is the purpose of an astronaut's backpack? (*to carry air and water*)

2. Why is a space suit necessary? (*It protects the astronaut from extreme temperatures and provides air for the astronaut to breathe.*)

3. Is the space suit heavy? (*Yes, but the astronaut doesn't feel the weight.*)

4. What other parts of a space suit are shown? (*camera, temperature control, helmet, glove, boot*)

Think Aloud

The title tells me that this diagram shows the parts of a space suit. Since I've never seen or used a space suit, I'm not familiar with its many parts. A diagram will help me learn each part of the suit and understand its importance. I'll read the information that goes with the arrows. These are the labels. This information will tell me facts about each part of a space suit.

Comprehension QuickCheck

You may use the following questions to check students' comprehension:

1. What are diagrams? (*special pictures that show the parts of something or how something works*)

2. Why are diagrams helpful? (*They illustrate a lot of information clearly and simply.*)

3. What does this diagram show? (*the parts of a space suit*)

4. What can you show using a diagram? Why? (*Answers will vary, but should be supported.*)

Diagrams

Many science books and articles contain **diagrams** to go with the text. A diagram is a special picture that shows the parts of something or how something works. The diagram helps you "picture" the information and makes it easier to understand.

Reading Tools

In this lesson, you will be reading a space article containing a diagram. Use the Reading Tools below to help you read a diagram.

- First, read the **title** and **introduction**. They tell you what the diagram is about. Look at the whole page. Notice how the information is presented.

- Look at the **labels**. These are important words to remember. They tell you the important parts of the diagram.

- Follow the **arrows**. The arrows connect the labels to the picture.

- Finally, look for **pronunciations**. They are sometimes provided and help you say new or difficult words.

Remember to use these Reading Tools when you read a diagram.

Space Suits

Space suits make it possible for astronauts (AS-truh-nawts) to survive in outer space. Space suits protect astronauts from very cold and very hot temperatures. They are filled with air so the astronauts can breathe.

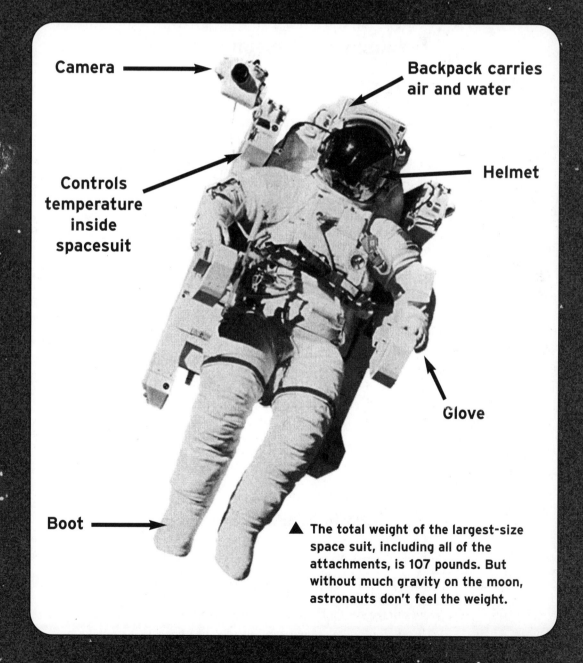

Camera

Backpack carries air and water

Controls temperature inside spacesuit

Helmet

Glove

Boot

▲ The total weight of the largest-size space suit, including all of the attachments, is 107 pounds. But without much gravity on the moon, astronauts don't feel the weight.

Reading "Living in Space"

M a t e r i a l s

▲ Student Text, "Living in Space," pp. 66–67

▲ Graphic Organizer p. 65

Teaching the Lesson

▲▲▲▲▲▲▲▲▲▲▲▲▲▲▲▲▲▲▲▲▲

Build Background

Distribute SmartChart Students will be reading about the building of a space station that will orbit Earth for many years. Distribute copies of the SmartChart, page 152, or create one on chart paper. Use the routine on page 21. Through your questioning, guide the discussion to identify students' knowledge and/or misconceptions about space stations.

Share Information Share with students the following information prior to reading:

✽ A space station is any permanent, inhabitable base that orbits the Earth.

✽ The first true space station, called Salyut 1, was launched by the Soviet Union on April 19, 1971. It was followed by several space stations, including Mir, which lasted until the 1990s.

✽ The first U.S. space station was Skylab. It was launched by NASA on May 14, 1973.

✽ In 1998, the United States and Russia joined to create the International Space Station. For the latest information on the International Space Station, visit NASA's Web site at www.spaceflight.nasa.gov/station/.

Preteach Vocabulary

Category Chart	Who?	Where?	How?
astronaut			
crew			
international			
planet			
solar system			

Preteach the following words from "Living in Space" using the Vocabulary Routine on page 26. Or you may wish to use the Category Chart shown at left. After they categorize the words, encourage students to share what they know about the words. The discussion will also give you an idea of how much knowledge students bring to the concepts they will be reading about.

As you read, help students define *orbit* by using context clues.

Define each word. Be sure to point out unusual pronunciations, multiple meanings, related words, and other aspects of the word.

☼ **astronaut** Someone who travels in space.

Explain that *astro* means "star" and *naut* means "sailor." Therefore, an astronaut "sails among the stars."

☼ **crew** A team of people who work together on a ship, aircraft, or a specific job.

Point out rhyming words *grew, true, blue,* and *do.*

☼ **international** Involving different countries.

Help students sound out the word by parts: in-ter-na-tion-al.

☼ **planet** One of the nine heavenly bodies circling the sun.

Name the nine planets for students. Teach them a mnemonic for remembering their names, such as **M**ary's **V**iolet **E**yes **M**ade **J**ohn **S**it **U**p **N**ear **P**luto.

☼ **solar system** The sun and the bodies that move in orbit around it, including moons, asteroids, comets, and planets.

Read the Selection

☼ Distribute copies of "Living in Space," pages 66–67. Have students preview the selection using the Preview Routine on page 39.

☼ Before the second reading, use the lesson below to teach students about the selection's text structure: compare and contrast.

Teaching the Text Structure:
Compare and Contrast

▲▲▲▲▲▲▲▲▲▲▲▲▲▲▲▲▲▲▲▲▲▲▲▲▲▲▲▲▲▲▲▲▲▲▲▲▲

Introduce Discuss the importance of identifying how text is structured. It alerts readers to how the text was written. This can help them organize their thinking as they read. Tell students that this article has many parts. Each part is organized in a special way. Direct students to the section called "Space Food Then and Now."

Model You may wish to use the Think Aloud at right as you model the compare and contrast structure of this part of the article.

Guided Practice/Apply As students reread the selection, have them complete the graphic organizer for compare and contrast, page 65. Then have students work in pairs to retell the information in their own words.

Think Aloud

Writers organize their writing in a way that helps us understand it. The title "Space Food Then and Now" tells me that we are going to compare what space food is like today and what it was like long ago. The way the text is chunked and the use of two photographs helps me understand how space food today and years ago is the same and how it is different.

Comprehension QuickCheck

Possible answers:

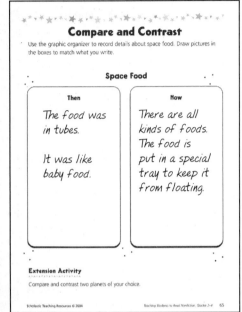

After you have completed the lesson, you may use the following questions to check students' comprehension:

1. Who is building the International Space Station? (*United States, Russia, and 14 other countries*)

2. What does *orbit* mean? (*to circle or go around, as in a planet orbiting the sun*)

3. What is space food like today? (*Astronauts eat all kinds of food today. It is served in special trays to prevent it from floating away.*)

4. How does the diagram help you understand our solar system? (*Answers will vary.*)

5. What other space-related object or process could you show in a diagram? (*Answers will vary.*)

Independent Practice: Writing

Have students write two or three sentences about the article. Have them include the following:

☀ the purpose of a space station,

☀ how astronauts live in space.

Web Links

www.kids-space.org/ — Kids Space

kids.earth.nasa.gov — NASA

starchild.gsfc.nasa.gov/docs/StarChild/StarChild.html — StarChild: A Learning Center for Young Astronomers

quest.arc.nasa.gov/ — NASA's Quest Project

Compare and Contrast

Use the graphic organizer to record details about space food. Draw pictures in the boxes to match what you write.

Space Food

Then

Now

Extension Activity

Compare and contrast two planets of your choice.

Living in Space

The best way to learn about space is to live there. Now, astronauts from around the world can do just that. The United States, Russia, and fourteen other countries are working together to build the **International Space Station**, or ISS.

Astronauts are building the ISS in space, piece by piece. It will take more than 40 trips to complete it. Astronauts have already started living there while it is being built. The first team moved to the ISS in November, 2000.

The International Space Station will look like this when it is fully built in 2006. It will be the size of two football fields.

These are the first astronauts to live on the International Space Station.

New Planets

There are nine planets in our solar system. They **orbit**, or circle, the sun. Now, experts have found 10 new planets in different solar systems.

Could there be life on these planets? Experts say the new planets are too far away from their suns to have life on them.

Our Solar System

Pluto

Neptune

Mercury

Uranus

Venus

Earth

Mars

Jupiter

Saturn

Sun

Look at the diagram above. In what ways is Saturn different from Earth?

Space Food News

Do you use a straw to drink? So do astronauts. Their straws have clamps on the ends. That's because everything floats in space—even liquids. The clamps keep the drink from floating up, up, and away!

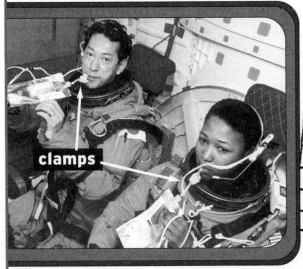

clamps

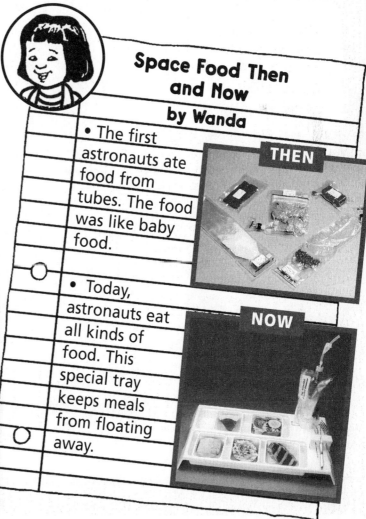

Space Food Then and Now
by Wanda

- The first astronauts ate food from tubes. The food was like baby food.

THEN

- Today, astronauts eat all kinds of food. This special tray keeps meals from floating away.

NOW

How to Read a Map

Spotlight

What Are Maps?

Help students understand that a map is a flat picture of Earth. There are five main types of maps: political, physical, landform, transportation, and historical.

- A **political map** shows information such as countries, states, cities, and capital cities. These maps are used to show the borders between large, organized areas.
- A **physical map** shows the Earth's natural features, such as mountains, oceans, and rivers. One type of physical map is the landform map.
- A **landform map** shows the shape of Earth's landmasses and bodies of water using colors and symbols. For example, bodies of water might be in blue and mountain ranges might be in various shades of brown to show elevation.
- A **transportation map** shows how you can travel from one place to another. Some transportation maps show major and minor roads that link cities and towns. Other transportation maps show bus, subway, train, boat, or airline routes.
- A **historical map** shows information about past events and places. These maps often show place names and political boundaries that differ from those today.

Why Are They Useful?

Maps are a visual way to represent a great deal of information in a limited space. Therefore, maps often use symbols instead of words. For example, a map may show a particular landform using a color or type of line, such as cross-hatching. Or, a map might show a city using a small circle or dot with the city's name written beside it. A capital city might be represented by a star inside a circle to distinguish it from other cities. Maps can help you visualize a place as you read about it.

Materials

▲ Reading Tools and Model Text, "Weather Watch," pp. 70–71

▲ Transparency 6

▲ Bookmark, p. 149

Teaching the Lesson

Direct Instruction

※ Distribute the Map lesson, pages 70–71. Have students read the information about maps silently before discussing the model text together and using the Reading Tools.

* Then, use the **color transparency** to guide students as they read and use the Reading Tools.

* Use the Minilesson below to teach the text feature.

Teaching the Text Feature

Introduce Maps Point out that a map contains clues that will help students read and understand it. To read maps, students should follow these steps:

* Read the **map title**. It tells readers what the map is about.
* Find the **symbols** on the map. A symbol is a picture or even a special color. It stands for a real thing or a real place.
* Look at the **map key**. It tells readers what each symbol on the map means.
* Read the **labels** on the map. These words tell the names of cities, states, countries, rivers, mountains, oceans, and other geographical places.
* Find the **compass rose**. It shows the directions on the map. **N** stands for north, **S** stands for south, **E** stands for east, and **W** stands for west.

Model Use the Think Aloud at right to model how to read a map.

Guided Practice/Apply Have students read "Weather Watch" on page 71 to learn about weather maps. Make sure they use the map's symbols and shading appropriately. Ask them to retell the information in their own words. You may also wish to ask the following:

1. Find our state. What was the weather where we live? (*Answers will vary.*)

2. What would the weather be like if you were in Phoenix? (*thunderstorms*)

3. Was it colder in Denver or Kansas City? (*Denver*)

4. What symbol was used to show warm, sunny weather? (*a sun with sunglasses*)

5. What other maps of the U.S. have you seen? What did they show? (*Answers will vary.*)

Think Aloud

The title tells me that this map shows the weather forecast for the United States on a particular day. Looking at the map key, I see that each type of weather has its own symbol. For example, I see that a smiling sun stands for a warm, sunny day with no rain. I also see the major cities identified by a small dot with the city's name written beside it. In addition, the outlines of each state are shown. This will help me find our state.

Comprehension QuickCheck

You may use the following questions to check students' comprehension:

1. What is a map? (*a flat representation of a place*)

2. Why is a map helpful? (*It can show a large place in a very small space. It can also help you find places.*)

3. What does this map show? (*the day's weather*)

4. If you wanted to draw a weather map for your state, which symbols would you use? Why? (*Answers will vary, but should be supported.*)

Map

A **map** is a flat picture of Earth. Imagine looking down on Earth from high in the sky. You would see the shapes of continents, large and small bodies of water, mountain ranges, and other natural features. There are five main types of maps: political, physical, landform, transportation, and historical. Each has a different use and special traits.

Reading Tools

In this lesson, you will be reading a U.S. weather map, one type of physical map. Use the Reading Tools below to help you read this type of map.

◉ Read the **map title**. It tells you what the map is about.

◉ Find the **symbols** on the map. A symbol is a picture or even a special color. It stands for a real thing or a real place.

◉ Look at the **map key** or **legend**. It tells you what each symbol on the map means.

◉ Read the **labels** on the map. These words tell the names of cities, states, countries, rivers, mountains, oceans, and other places.

◉ Find the **compass rose**. It shows the directions on the map. **N** stands for north, **S** stands for south, **E** stands for east, and **W** stands for west.

Remember to use these Reading Tools when you read a map.

Weather Watch

A weather map shows the weather in different places.

March 7

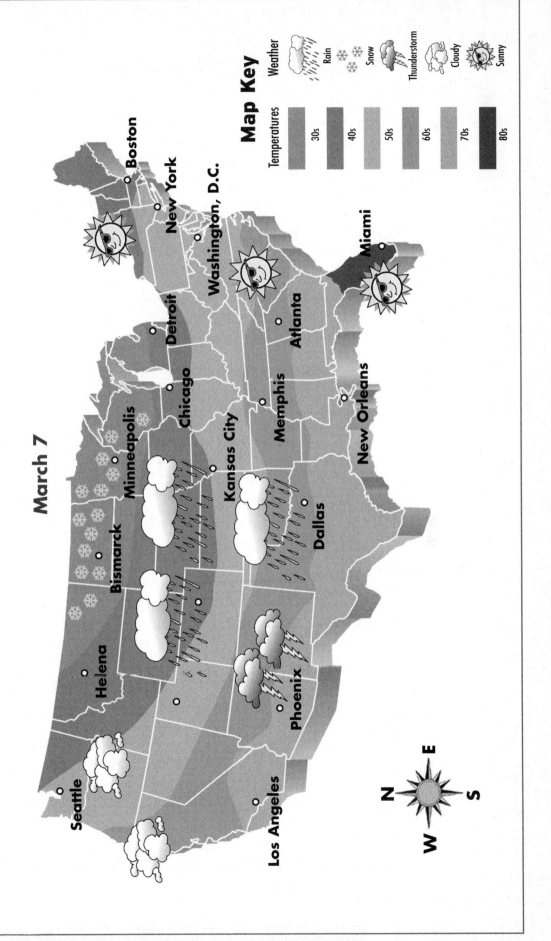

Map Key

Weather: Rain, Snow, Thunderstorm, Cloudy, Sunny

Temperatures: 30s, 40s, 50s, 60s, 70s, 80s

Cities: Boston, New York, Washington, D.C., Miami, Detroit, Atlanta, Chicago, Memphis, New Orleans, Minneapolis, Kansas City, Dallas, Bismarck, Helena, Phoenix, Seattle, Los Angeles

Compass: N, E, S, W

Reading "What Is Congress?"

M a t e r i a l s

▲ Student Text, "What Is Congress?," pp. 76–77

▲ Graphic Organizer p. 75

Teaching the Lesson

Build Background

Distribute SmartChart Students will be viewing a physical map of the United States and reading information about the congressional members from each state. Distribute copies of the SmartChart, page 152, or create one on chart paper. Use the routine on page 21. Through your questioning, guide the discussion to identify students' knowledge and/or misconceptions about Congress and lawmaking.

Share Information You may wish to share the following:

* ❅ Congress is our legislative branch of government. Congress makes our country's laws.

* ❅ Congress is made up of two parts—the Senate and the House of Representatives.

Preteach Vocabulary

Preteach the following words from "What Is Congress?" using the Vocabulary Routine on page 26. Or you may wish to use the chart shown at left. Encourage students to share what they know about each category. The discussion will also give you an idea of how much knowledge students bring to the concepts they will be reading about.

Define each word. Be sure to point out unusual pronunciations, related words, and other aspects of the word.

* ❅ **laws** A rule made by the government that must be obeyed. Connect to the word *rules*.

* ❅ **elect** To choose someone or decide something by voting. Connect to the words *vote* and *election*.

* ❅ **Congress** The government body of the U.S. that makes laws.

Knowledge Chart

What We Do	Who Are They?	What They Do
(elect)	(Congress)	(make laws)
	(senators)	
	(representatives)	

✸ **senators** A member of the U.S Senate, serving six-year terms.

✸ **representatives** Members of the U.S. House of Representatives, serving two-year terms.

Read the Selection

✸ Distribute copies of "What Is Congress?," pages 76–77. Have students preview the selection using the Preview Routine on page 39. Then, guide students as they apply the strategies they have learned for navigating text. Remind students to use the Reading Tools to read the map provided.

✸ Before the second reading, use the Minilesson below to teach students about the selection's text structure: compare and contrast.

Teaching the Text Structure:
Compare and Contrast

Introduce Discuss the importance of identifying how text is structured. It alerts readers to how the text was written. This can help them organize their thinking as they read. Tell students that this article tells the difference between the two parts of Congress—the Senate and the House of Representatives. It compares them, telling how they are alike. It also contrasts them, telling how they are different.

Model You may wish to use the Think Aloud at right as you model the text structure of "What Is Congress?"

Guided Practice/Apply As students reread the selection, have them complete the graphic organizer for compare and contrast, page 75. Then have students work in pairs to retell the information in their own words.

Think Aloud

Writers organize their writing in a way that helps us understand it. The author of this article compares the two groups that make up Congress— the Senate and the House of Representatives. These are the people who make our laws. We will learn how they are alike and how they are different.

Comprehension QuickCheck

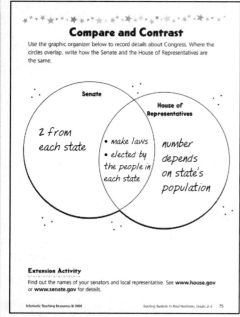

Possible answers:

After you have completed the lesson, you may use the following questions to check students' comprehension:

1. What is Congress? (*The group in government that makes our laws.*)

2. Are there more representatives or senators? (*representatives*)

3. Which state has more representatives—New Hampshire or Texas? Why? (*Texas. It has more people.*)

4. Where is your state on the map? (*Answers will vary.*)

5. How does the map help you learn about Congress? (*You can see which states are larger, and therefore might have more people and more representatives.*)

Independent Practice: Writing

Have students write two or three sentences about Congress. Suggest that they use the graphic organizer they completed while reading to help them create their summaries. Have them include the following:

☀ a description of Congress,

☀ the difference between the Senate and House of Representatives.

Web Links

teacher.scholastic.com/fieldtrip/science/weather.htm
                    Scholastic Weather Center Resources

bensguide.gpo.gov   Ben's Guide to American Government

www.mapquest.com   MapQuest

www.nationalgeographic.com/maps   National Geographic Maps

www.3datlas.com   3D Atlas Online

www.50states.com   U.S. States

www.wildweather.com   Dan's Wild Weather Page

www.whitehouse.gov   The White House

www.civnet.org/resources/teach/lessplan/student1.htm
                    We the People

Compare and Contrast

Use the graphic organizer below to record details about Congress. Where the circles overlap, write how the Senate and the House of Representatives are the same.

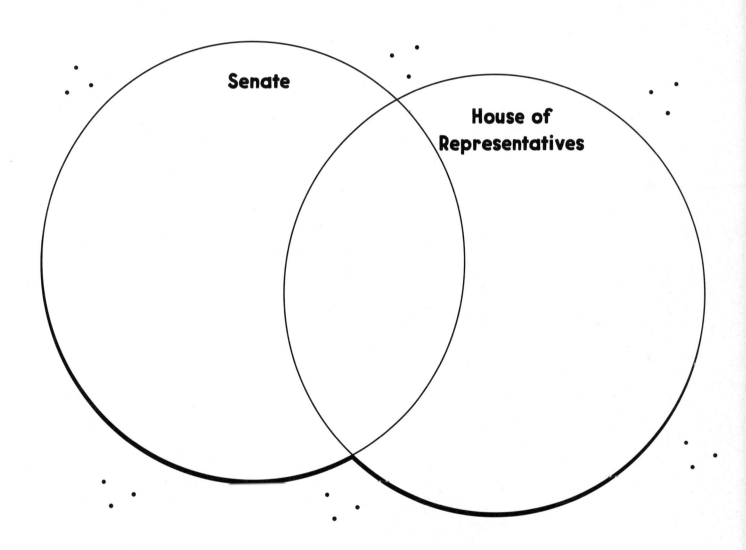

Senate

House of Representatives

Extension Activity

Find out the names of your senators and local representative. See www.house.gov or www.senate.gov for details.

What Is Congress?

What Does Congress Do?

Congress makes laws for our country. This is one of its most important jobs. Some of our laws are about crime and safety. Other laws are about taxes and money.

The U.S. ▶
Congressional
Seal

UNITED STATES CONGRESS

▲ Congress meets
in the Capitol
Building in
Washington, D.C.

Members of ▶
Congress meet
with people
from their
state to find
out what the
people want.

Who Is in Congress?

Congress is made up of two groups of people. The two groups are the Senate and the House of Representatives. The people of every state elect two senators. They also elect members of the House of Representatives. The number of representatives for each state depends on how many people live there.

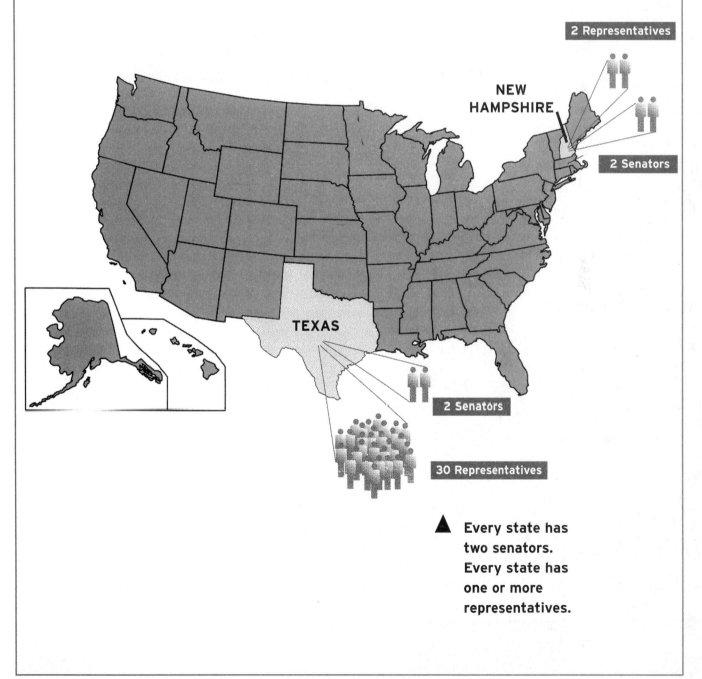

2 Representatives

NEW HAMPSHIRE

2 Senators

TEXAS

2 Senators

30 Representatives

▲ Every state has two senators. Every state has one or more representatives.

How to Read a Flow Chart

Spotlight

What Are Flow Charts?

A flow chart is a kind of diagram. Flow charts often accompany nonfiction, or expository texts, so students will encounter them in both their science and social studies reading. A flow chart in your science textbook may illustrate a concept, such as the life cycle of a plant or animal. In a social studies book, a flow chart may show a sequence of steps, such as the production of bread or how a law is passed.

Why Are They Useful?

It's important for students to know how a flow chart can help them to read nonfiction. Sometimes an explanation is complicated and difficult to follow. A flow chart shows the same information that's in the text, but it does so visually. The flow chart helps the reader visualize the text, thereby making the text easier to understand and remember.

Materials

▲ Reading Tools and Model Text, "How a Butterfly Grows," pp. 80–81

▲ Transparency 7

▲ Bookmark, p. 149

Teaching the Lesson

Direct Instruction

❋ Distribute the Flow Chart lesson, pages 80–81. Have students read the information about flow charts silently before discussing the model text together and using the Reading Tools.

❋ Then display the **color transparency** and use it to guide students as they read and use the Reading Tools.

❋ Use the Minilesson to teach the text feature, a flow chart.

Teaching the Text Feature

Introduce Flow Charts Tell students that a flow chart is an illustration that shows the order in which something happens, step by step. Why might an article include a flow chart? Because a flow chart helps readers picture clearly what they read about.

Explain that when they see a flow chart, students should:

- read the **title** to learn what the flow chart is about.
- use the **numbers** and **arrows** to follow the steps in their correct order.
- study the **pictures, labels,** and **explanations**.
- look for **special features**, such as boldfaced words and pronunciations.

Model Use the Think Aloud at right to model how you read a flow chart.

Guided Practice/Apply Help students read "How a Butterfly Grows" on page 81. Make sure they are able to read the flow chart in the correct order. Then ask them to retell the information in their own words.

Think Aloud

The title tells me that this flow chart shows how a butterfly grows. The flow chart has four steps. Each one is numbered. I start with number 1, study the picture, and read the label and the explanation. When I'm finished, I follow the arrow to the next number. That way I read each step in the correct order.

When I see a boldfaced word, I try to remember it. When I see a pronunciation, I practice saying the word.

Comprehension QuickCheck

You may use the following questions to check students' comprehension.

1. What is a flow chart, and why is it helpful? (*It is a diagram that shows the order in which something happens; it illustrates what you are reading and helps you better understand it.*)

2. What does this flow chart show? (*how a butterfly grows*)

3. What happens after the caterpillar hatches and eats all day? (*It grows a hard skin.*)

4. How do you pronounce the word c-h-r-y-s-a-l-i-s? (*KRIS-uh-lis*)

5. What information might *you* explain using a flow chart? (*Answers will vary, but should be appropriate for the function of a flow chart.*)

Read About Science

Flow Chart

Science books sometimes explain how living things grow and change. Take a look at the article on page 81. It describes how a butterfly grows. Notice the illustration. It shows each step in the amazing change from an egg to an adult butterfly. This kind of illustration is called a **flow chart**. A flow chart might also be used to show how a car is made or how beavers build a dam.

A flow chart shows all the steps of an activity in the order they happen. Flow charts make it easier for you to understand what you read. It's really important to follow the steps in the correct order. Otherwise you might think that the windows of the car go in before the body is put together!

Reading Tools

Use the tools below to read a flow chart.

- First read the **title**. It tells you what the flow chart is about.

- Next, look at the **numbers**. They tell you the order of the steps. Always start at number 1.

- Notice that each step has a **picture** and a **label**. Read the label and study the picture.

- Read the **explanation** for each step. It gives you important information.

- Follow the **arrow**. It will take you to the next step.

- Notice the **boldfaced words**. These are important vocabulary to remember.

- Look for **pronunciations**. They help you say new or difficult words.

Remember to use these Reading Tools when you see a flow chart in your reading.

How a Butterfly Grows

Butterflies look different from each other. But all butterflies grow and change in the same way. This is called a **life cycle** (life SYE-kuhl).

4 steps in a butterfly's life cycle.

START HERE →

Step 1. A butterfly lays an **egg**. In real life, the egg is as tiny as this dot. •

Step 2. A **caterpillar** hatches from the egg. Time to eat. The hungry caterpillar gobbles up leaves all day.

Step 3. Then the caterpillar grows a hard skin around itself. The skin is called a **chrysalis** (KRIS-uh-lis).

Step 4. The caterpillar changes inside the chrysalis. Look at what comes out of the chrysalis. A **butterfly**!

butterfly

chrysalis

caterpillar

egg

M a t e r i a l s

▲ Student Text,
  "How Amphibians
  Grow and Change,"
  pp. 86–87

▲ Graphic Organizer
  p. 85

Reading "How Amphibians Grow and Change"

Teaching the Lesson

Build Background

Distribute SmartChart Students will be reading a chapter of a science textbook about metamorphosis. Distribute copies of the SmartChart, page 152, or create one on chart paper. Use the routine on page 21. Through your questioning, guide the discussion to identify students' knowledge and/or misconceptions about amphibians and how they grow.

Share Information The gaps in your students' prior knowledge (the "What We Know" column) should determine which of the following background information you share with them before they begin reading.

   ❋ An amphibian is a cold-blooded animal that begins its life in water, but is able to live both on land and in water later in its life.

   ❋ Frogs, toads, and salamanders are three kinds of amphibians.

Preteach Vocabulary

Preteach the words below from "How Amphibians Grow and Change" using the Vocabulary Routine on page 26. Or you may wish to use the Word Map shown on the next page.

   Present each word and provide a context sentence. Define the word. Also point out pronunciations and word origins. As you read, help students define *metamorphosis*, *froglet*, and *hind legs* by using the context clues in the text.

   ❋ **amphibian** A cold-blooded animal that can live in water and on land. *Frogs and toads are amphibians.*

Go over the pronunciation of *amphibian;* call students' attention to the letters *ph* that stand for the sound /f/. Point out that the word *amphibian* comes from two Greek words that mean "both" and "life." Amphibians can live both in water and on land.

❋ **life cycle** The changes that every living thing goes through as it develops from an egg to an adult. *A butterfly changes its form as it goes through its life cycle.*

❋ **gills** An organ through which fish and other animals that live in water breathe. *A fish gets oxygen from water through its gills.*

Read the Selection

❋ Distribute copies of "How Amphibians Grow and Change," pages 86–87.

❋ Before the second reading, use the Minilesson to teach students about the selection's text structure: sequence.

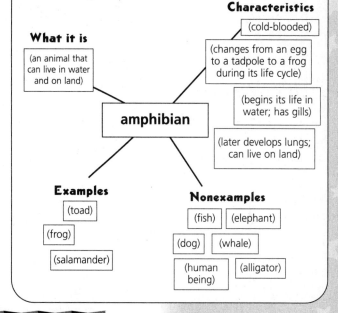

Word Map

Draw the word map shown below on the board or on a sheet of paper that can be saved. As you discuss the vocabulary words, have students fill in the map. Students can add concepts after they have completed their reading.

Characteristics
(cold-blooded)
(changes from an egg to a tadpole to a frog during its life cycle)
(begins its life in water; has gills)
(later develops lungs; can live on land)

What it is
(an animal that can live in water and on land)

amphibian

Examples
(toad)
(frog)
(salamander)

Nonexamples
(fish) (elephant)
(dog) (whale)
(human being) (alligator)

Teaching the Text Structure: Sequence

Introduce Remind students that a writer organizes nonfiction in several ways called text structures. Writers may:

- **compare and contrast** two people, places, or things;
- **describe** someone or something;
- tell the **sequence**, or order, in which something happens;
- tell about a **problem and its solution**; or
- explain the **cause and effect** of something.

Explain that knowing how a text is organized will help students better understand and remember the information.

Model Use the Think Aloud at right as you model how to determine that the text structure of "How Amphibians Grow and Change" is sequence.

Guided Practice/Apply As students reread, help them complete the circle organizer on page 85. Then have students work with a partner to give an oral explanation of the metamorphosis of a frog. Students may use their graphic organizers for reference.

T h i n k A l o u d

As I read "How Amphibians Grow and Change," I look for clues that show how the writer organized the information. I see the words in about ten days, about five weeks later, after that, *and* finally. *These words are clues that the writer is telling me about a sequence. I know I'm going to read about the steps in the life cycle of a frog, so as I read, I'll look for each step.*

I also see a flow chart that shows all the steps in the order they happen. The pictures help me understand the order. Filling out a graphic organizer helps me remember the steps in the right order.

Possible answers:

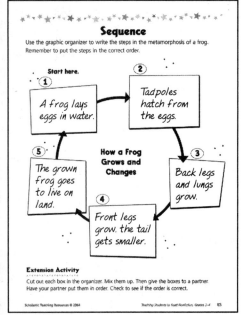

After you have completed the lesson, you may use the following questions to check students' comprehension:

1. How did the flow chart in this selection help you? (*It shows pictures of each step in the metamorphosis of a frog and the order in which the steps happen. The flow chart helps you understand and remember the steps.*)

2. What makes it possible for a tadpole to live in water? (*gills*)

3. What makes it possible for a frog to live on land? (*lungs instead of gills; also front and hind legs for moving*)

4. How is the life cycle of a frog different from the life cycle of a cat? (*A cat grows as it gets older, but it doesn't change its form as a frog does.*)

Independent Practice: Writing

Have each student write a brief autobiography of a frog. The autobiography may be fanciful (e.g., the student may give the frog a name and an address, such as Froggie Pond), but it should include the correct facts about metamorphosis.

www.sandiegozoo.org   San Diego Zoo
www.exploratorium.edu/frogs   The Exploratorium's Frog Exhibition

Sequence

Use the graphic organizer to write the steps in the metamorphosis of a frog. Remember to put the steps in the correct order.

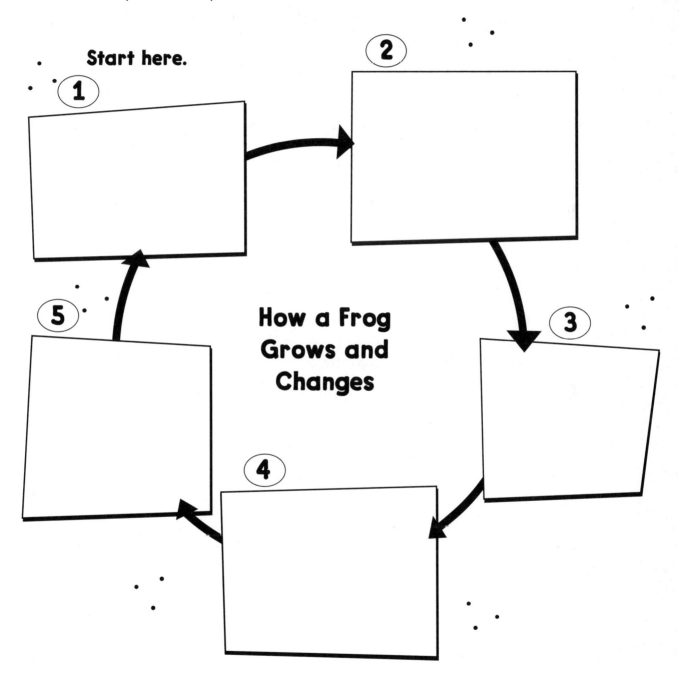

Start here.

1

2

3

4

5

How a Frog Grows and Changes

Extension Activity

Cut out each box in the organizer. Mix them up. Then give the boxes to a partner. Have your partner put them in order. Check to see if the order is correct.

How Amphibians Grow and Change

Amphibians change their form as they grow. This change is called **metamorphosis** (met-uh-MORE-fuh-sis). Metamorphosis means "to change form." For example, a frog changes from a tadpole to an adult frog. The whole process takes from 12 to 14 weeks, or about three and a half months. This process is called the frog's life cycle. Here's what happens.

A frog begins its life in water, where the adult frog lays its eggs. In about ten days, the egg hatches, and a tadpole wiggles out. Tadpoles have a tail for swimming and gills for breathing underwater.

About five weeks later, the gills disappear, and the tadpole grows lungs. Now it breathes air. This means that the tadpole has to swim to the surface of the pond for air.

After that, the tadpole grows back legs and then front legs. As the tadpole grows and changes, its tail disappears. Finally, the tadpole becomes a froglet, or a young frog. Now it can leave the water.

In about three years, the full-grown frog will be ready to lay eggs. It will return to the water, and the cycle will start all over again!

How a Frog Grows

1 A frog lays its eggs in water.

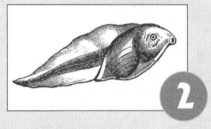

2 Tadpoles hatch from the eggs. They live in the water and breathe through gills.

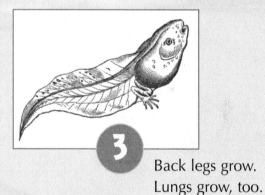

3 Back legs grow. Lungs grow, too.

4 Front legs grow. The tail shrinks.

5 The grown frog lives on land. It breathes through its lungs.

How to Read a Magazine Article

Spotlight

What Are Magazine Articles?

Magazine articles are nonfiction sources that are published in a periodical at regular intervals—usually weekly or monthly. They contain factual information about a specific topic and one or more of the following features: quotes about the topic from people who were interviewed, photographs, illustrations, and graphic aids such as graphs and diagrams.

Why Are They Useful?

Magazine articles tend to be short, specialized, and written at a high-interest level. They provide current information in an abbreviated form. Many contain first-hand accounts of events.

Materials

▲ Reading Tools and Model Text, "The U.S. Welcomes Latinos," pp. 90–91

▲ Transparency 8

▲ Bookmark, p. 149

Teaching the Lesson

Direct Instruction

❋ Distribute the Magazine Article lesson, pages 90–91. Have students read the information about magazines silently before discussing the model text together and using the Reading Tools.

❋ Then display the **color transparency** and use it to guide students as they read and use the Reading Tools.

❋ Use the Minilesson on page 89 to teach students how to read a graph.

Teaching the Text Feature

Introduce Graphs Explain to students that a graph is a drawing. It shows number information about a particular topic. A circle graph is also called a pie graph. It shows how something can be divided into parts or "slices," just like a pie. By looking at the pie graph, readers can quickly tell which "slice" is the biggest, which one is the smallest, and which slices are in between. It's like dividing up an apple pie and comparing each person's slice. Who got the biggest piece? Who got the smallest?

Model You may wish to use the Think Aloud at right to model how to read the pie graph.

Guided Practice/Apply Have students reread "The U.S. Welcomes Latinos" and study the pie graph. Ask them to rank the countries that Latinos came from 1 to 5, with 1 as the place where most Latinos came from.

Comprehension QuickCheck

After you have completed the lesson, you may use the following questions to check students' comprehension.

1. What country do most Latinos come from? (*Mexico*)

2. Which is the second largest slice of the pie? What place does it stand for? (*Puerto Rico*)

3. What country do the fewest Latinos come from? (*Dominican Republic*)

4. Do more Latinos come from Cuba or El Salvador? (*Cuba*)

5. What country might be included in the slice labeled "Other"? (*Answers will vary, but should include Spanish-speaking countries.*)

6. If you had to tell a classmate about pie graphs, what would you say? (*Answers should reflect a clear understanding of how to read a pie graph.*)

The title of the pie graph tells me that it is about Latinos who live in the United States. It shows the top five places where Latinos originally came from. The slice labeled "Other" stands for <u>all</u> the other countries in South America, Central America, and the Caribbean that Latinos came from— like Peru, Guatemala, and Haiti.

The graph gives me information at a glance. A quick look is all it takes to show me that the biggest slice of the pie stands for Mexico. That's because more Latinos in the U.S. came from Mexico than any other country.

When I read the graph, I can also make comparisons. I see that more Latinos came from Puerto Rico than from the Dominican Republic.

Magazines

Imagine you're relaxing in a comfortable chair. Or taking a long bus ride. Or doing research for a report you have to write. What might you be reading? A **magazine**.

A magazine comes out at regular times—like every week or every month. Magazine articles are usually short pieces of nonfiction that contain many facts about a topic. They may also include quotes from people the writer spoke to. You'll find interviews, photographs, graphs, and many other features in them, too.

Just be sure your magazine is up-to-date. That way you'll get the latest scoop about people, places, and events.

Reading Tools

In this lesson, you will read a magazine article. Use the Reading Tools to help you.

◎ Read the **headline** to find out what the article is about.

◎ Read each **heading**. It tells you the main idea of the section that you're about to read. You'll know what to expect.

◎ Say to yourself, **"This article will be about . . . ."**

◎ As you read, use the **pronunciations**. They tell you how to say certain words.

◎ Try to remember **boldfaced words**. They are important vocabulary words.

◎ Look carefully at any **photographs** and **graphs**. They give you more information.

◎ Be sure to read the **captions**, too. They explain what the photos and diagrams show.

Remember to use these Reading Tools when you read magazine articles.

The U.S. Welcomes Latinos

When she was 8 years old, Belén Vasquez (Beh-LEHN VAHS-kehs) made a big move. She and her parents moved to the U.S. from Mexico. Belén spoke only Spanish when she arrived. Now she reads and writes in both Spanish and English.

Belén is one of 35 million Latinos (lah-TEE-nohs) living in the U.S. They are the largest minority group in the country.

Celebrating Hispanic Heritage

Latinos, also called Hispanics, share the Spanish language. But they come from more than 20 countries in North, Central, and South America, and the Caribbean. They bring customs and foods from their native countries. For example, if you eat a taco, you

"My teacher and classmates helped me when I didn't understand English," says Belén.

are tasting a treat from Belén's country, Mexico.

Hispanic Heritage Month is observed from September 15 to October 15. It is a way to say, "Thank you, Latinos, for sharing your **heritage**."

READ A CIRCLE GRAPH

Latinos in the U.S.

This is a circle graph or "pie graph." It shows the top five places where Latinos living in the U.S. come from. The biggest piece of the pie stands for Mexico. That's because most Latinos come to the U.S. from Mexico.

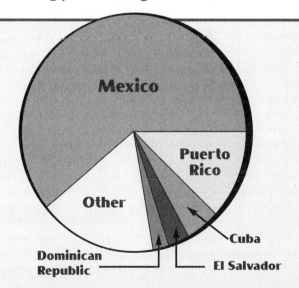

Reading "Meet Gary Soto"

Materials

▲ Student Text, "Meet Gary Soto," pp. 96–97

▲ Graphic Organizer p. 95

Teaching the Lesson

Build Background

Distribute SmartChart Students will be reading an interview with author Gary Soto. Distribute copies of the SmartChart, page 152, or create one on chart paper. Use the routine on page 21. Through your questioning, guide the discussion to identify students' prior knowledge about Gary Soto and about interviews.

Share Information The gaps in your students' prior knowledge (the "What We Know" column) should determine which of the following background information you share with them before they begin reading.

✵ Gary Soto's family came to the United States from Mexico. He lives in Berkeley, California. He writes stories and poetry for both children and adults. He has also written the libretto (the words that are sung) for an opera.

✵ An interview is a conversation between two people—an interviewer and the person being interviewed. The interviewer asks questions about specific information. The person being interviewed answers the questions. An interview gives the reader a sense of meeting the person who is being interviewed.

✵ An interview has a special format: it leads off with the question which is followed by the answer. The interviewer and the person being interviewed are identified by name or initials. In "Meet Gary Soto," the initials "SN" stand for Scholastic News and "GS" for Gary Soto.

Preteach Vocabulary

Preteach the following words from "Meet Gary Soto" using the Vocabulary Routine on page 26. Or you may wish to use the "What's the Connection?" chart shown at left.

What's the Connection?

Draw the chart pictured below. Have students think about how each pair of words go together. Ask them to fill in the chart with a sentence or phrase that explains the relationship.

Words	How they go together
writer poet	(A poet is a writer.)
inspire coach	(A good coach makes a team want to win.)
memories photos	(Photos help you remember things.)
bilingual bicycle	(2 languages 2 wheels)

Present each word and provide a context sentence. Define the word. Also point out synonyms, related words, prefixes, and other aspects of the word. As you read, help students define *tragic* and *exclusively* by using the context clues in the text.

✵ **inspire** Give a person the feeling of wanting to do something well. *The teacher inspires her students to do well.*

✵ **memories** What a person remembers. *I have great memories of our trip to a farm.*

 Point out that when you *memorize* something like a poem, you put it in your memory.

✵ **bilingual** Able to speak two languages. *Shen Ching is bilingual. She speaks English and Chinese.*

 Point out the prefix *bi-*, meaning two. Other words with this prefix are *bicycle*, a machine that has two wheels and *binoculars*, an object that is used with both eyes to see things that are far away.

✵ **poet** A person who writes poems. *Shel Silverstein is a very funny poet.* Related words are *poem* and *poetry*.

Read the Selection

✵ Distribute copies of "Meet Gary Soto," pages 96–97. Guide them in reading the interview and the poem and in interpreting the graph.

✵ Before the second reading, use the Minilesson below to teach students about the selection's text structure: description.

Teaching the Text Structure: Description

Introduce Remind students that writers of nonfiction often organize their writing in one of five ways: description, sequence, compare and contrast, cause and effect, problem and solution. Knowing how the writing is organized helps readers understand and remember what they read.

Model You may wish to use the Think Aloud at right as you model how to determine the text structure of the article: description.

Guided Practice/Apply As students reread the selection, have them fill out the Gary Soto Fact Sheet, page 95. Then have them orally summarize the information.

Think Aloud

In the interview Gary Soto describes how he writes. He tells where he gets his ideas from. He describes how he uses Spanish and English in his writing. Also, he describes what you should do if you want to become a writer.

As I read, I find out what Gary Soto says about himself and his writing. His descriptions will help me understand and remember the information.

Possible answers:

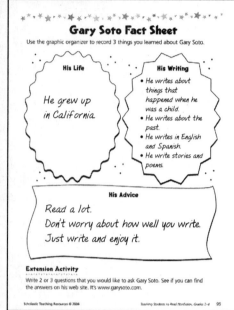

After you have completed the lesson, you may use the following questions to check students' comprehension:

1. Where does Gary Soto get many of his ideas for his stories and poems? *(from things that happened to him in his childhood)*

2. Where did he get his idea for the poem? *(from the time he found a cat on the street)*

3. How does Gary Soto use his bilingual knowledge? *(He uses Spanish words and expressions in his writing.)*

4. What is Gary Soto's most popular book with second and third graders? *(Too Many Tamales)*

5. What books by Gary Soto have you read? Which one did you like the best? *(Answers will vary.)*

Independent Practice: Writing

Have each student read one of the books that appears in the graph. Then have them write a brief book report about it. They should summarize the story and tell how they liked it.

www.garysoto.com	Gary Soto
www.americaslibrary.gov	"America's Story" from the Library of Congress
www.mexonline.com/culture.htm	Mexico Art and Culture Directory
www.ellisisland.org	Ellis Island
teacher.scholastic.com/fieldtrp/socstu.htm	Scholastic

Gary Soto Fact Sheet

Use the graphic organizer to record 3 things you learned about Gary Soto.

His Life

His Writing

His Advice

Extension Activity

Write 2 or 3 questions that you would like to ask Gary Soto. See if you can find the answers on his web site. It's **www.garysoto.com**.

MEET GARY SOTO

Gary Soto is a Mexican-American author who writes about growing up in California. Scholastic News talked to Gary Soto about his writing.

SN: What inspires you to write?

GS: Childhood memories, both funny and **tragic** or sad. I write about what happened in the past, not what is happening now.

SN: When do you use Spanish instead of English?

GS: Most authors work **exclusively** in one language, but I work in English, sprinkling it with Spanish. I use Spanish for the common and useful phrases that are part of everyday life, like *¡Mira!* (Look!), and *¡Cállate!* (Be quiet!)

Gary Soto reads his book *Too Many Tamales* **to some friends.**

SN: What is it like to be bilingual?

GS: Knowing two languages helps you to know more about the world. To laugh in two languages is cool. To dream in two languages is very cool.

SN: What advice do you have for children who want to become writers?

GS: Books are beautiful to hold and beautiful to read. Start your own library and read as much as you can. As for writing, don't worry about doing it well the first time, just play and enjoy. *¡Buena suerte!* (Good luck!)

GARY SOTO'S MOST POPULAR BOOKS

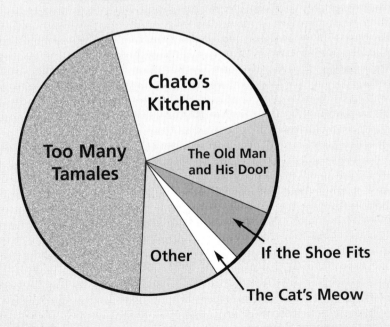

ODE TO MI GATO*

Here is an excerpt from Gary's poem, "Ode to Mi Gato."

. . . I love mi gato,
Porque* I found
Him on the fender
Of an abandoned car.
He was a kitten,
With a meow
Like the rusty latch
On a gate. I carried
Him home in my arms.
I poured milk
Into him, let him
Lick chunks of
Cheese from my palms,
And cooked huevo*
After huevo
Until his purring
Engine kicked in
And he cuddled
　Up to my father's slippers . . .

mi gato is Spanish for "my cat"
porque means "because"
huevo is Spanish for "egg"

How to Read a Time Line

Spotlight

What Are Time Lines?

A time line is a special type of diagram. A time line shows a series of events and the dates on which they happened.

Why Are They Useful?

Time lines can show events in a visually simple way. For example, a time line can show the major historical events in one century—all on one page. Time lines often span large amounts of time and show relationships between and among events.

Materials

▲ Reading Tools and Model Text, "A Century of Hits," pp. 100–101

▲ Transparency 9

▲ Bookmark, p. 149

Teaching the Lesson

Direct Instruction

☼ Distribute the Time Line lesson, pages 100–101. Have students read the information about time lines silently before discussing the model text together and using the Reading Tools.

☼ Then, use the **color transparency** to guide students as they read and use the Reading Tools.

☼ Use the Minilesson on page 99 to teach the text feature.

Teaching the Text Feature

Introduce Time Lines Point out that time lines are a special type of graphic aid that shows a series of events and the dates on which they happened. To read time lines students should:

- First, read the **title** of the time line. It tells readers the topic or historical period covered in the time line.
- Read the **introduction** (also called a **deck**) if there is one. It is the text above the time line and often provides background information about the topic of the time line.
- Find the starting and ending **dates** for the time line. Some time lines, like this one, are horizontal. They are read from left to right. Other time lines are vertical. These are read from the top to the bottom of the page.
- Read the **labels** for each date. They describe each event.

Model Use the Think Aloud at right to model how to read the time line.

Guided Practice/Apply Have students read "A Century of Hits" on page 101 to learn about popular book and TV series. Make sure they read the time line from left to right and can connect each date to a label. Ask them to retell the information in their own words. You may also wish to ask the following:

1. What place and time period are covered in this time line? (*the 1900s*)
2. What popular book character was created in 1962? (*Clifford*)
3. Which character appeared first—Amelia Bedelia or Charlie Brown? (*Charlie Brown*)
4. When was your favorite character created? (*Answers will vary.*)

T h i n k   A l o u d

The title tells me that this time line covers a specific topic—the "hits," or popular book and TV characters throughout the past century. I begin reading the time line on the left. There I see 1900. That's when the time period begins. In 1902, I read that the popular book The Tale of Peter Rabbit *was written. As I continue reading the time line from left to right, I will learn when other book and TV characters were created.*

Comprehension QuickCheck

You may use the following questions to check students' comprehension:

1. What are time lines? (*diagrams that show when events happened*)
2. Why are time lines helpful? (*They provide information about a lot of events in a small space.*)
3. What does this time line show? (*the most popular book and TV characters during the 1900s*)
4. If you wanted to create a time line about the past year, what information would you include and why? (*Answers will vary but should be supported.*)

Time Lines

What happened? and *When?* are two questions you might ask yourself when learning about a new topic or time period. For example, you might want to know what happened in the U.S. in the 1900s. To find out, you could look at a **time line**.

A time line is a special type of diagram. It shows a series of events and the years in which they happened. This information is always presented in time order. Time lines contain a lot of information in a limited space, making it easy to learn about a time period at a glance.

Reading Tools

In this lesson, you will be reading a time line. Use the Reading Tools below to help you read it.

◎ First, read the **title** of the time line. It tells you the topic of the time line.

◎ Sometimes there is an **introduction**. It explains what kind of information you will find on the time line.

◎ Find the starting and ending **dates**. They tell you how much time is covered. All the dates in between appear in time order. They tell you the year when each event took place.

◎ Finally, read the **labels** for each date. They describe, or tell more information about, each event.

Remember to use these Reading Tools when you read time lines.

A CENTURY of Hits

2000

1990

1980

1970

1960

1950

1940

1900

1981

Julian

Where do stories come from? Author Ann Cameron got some of hers from the true adventures of her friend, Julian DeWetts.

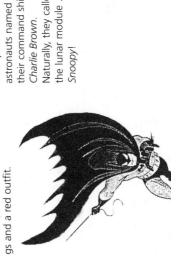

1998

Harry Potter

This amazing boy rocketed to fame during his first year at Hogwarts School. Now everyone is wild about Harry.

1988

Ms. Frizzle

The Friz drove the Magic School Bus right off the page and onto your television screen.

1962

Clifford

Talk about big! This red dog isn't just a book and video. He's a giant balloon in New York's Thanksgiving Day Parade.

1963

Amelia Bedelia

Who but Amelia Bedelia would put sponges in sponge cake? The author, that's who! She tried out all of Amelia's recipes.

1950

Charlie Brown

The *Apollo 10* astronauts named their command ship *Charlie Brown*. Naturally, they called the lunar module . . . *Snoopy!*

1939

Batman

Batman didn't start out with his trademark cape and costume. At first, the artist drew him with stiff bat's wings and a red outfit.

1902

Peter Rabbit

The Tale of Peter Rabbit hopped to fame as the best-selling children's book ever.

Reading "My Millennium Time Line"

Teaching the Lesson

Build Background

Distribute SmartChart Students will be reading a time line detailing an important or interesting invention in each century throughout the past millennium. Distribute copies of the SmartChart, page 152, or create one on chart paper. Use the routine on page 21. Through your questioning, guide the discussion to identify students' knowledge and/or misconceptions about the technology of long ago.

Share Information You may wish to share the following:

☀ A millennium lasts for 1,000 years.

☀ The last millennium lasted from the year 1000 to the year 2000.

☀ Many things we use today were invented hundreds of years ago.

Preteach Vocabulary

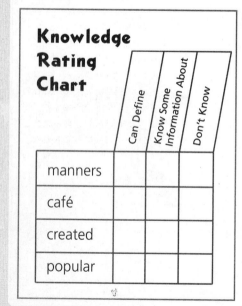

Preteach the following words from "My Millennium Time Line" using the Vocabulary Routine on page 26. Or you may wish to use the Knowledge Rating chart shown at left. After each student rates his or her knowledge of the words, follow up with a discussion of which words are the easiest, most difficult, and most unfamiliar to the greatest number of students. Encourage students to share what they know about the words. The discussion will also give you an idea of how much knowledge students bring to the concepts they will be reading about.

Define each word. Be sure to point out additional multiple meanings, related words including synonyms, multiple pronunciations, and other aspects of the word.

❋ **manners** The way in which someone behaves. *It is important to use your best manners when eating at a restaurant.*

❋ **café** A small restaurant. *The couple sat in the café and drank coffee.*

❋ **created** Made. *We created a new gadget for cleaning the floor.*

❋ **popular** Well-liked. *Pizza is the most popular food at our school.*

Read the Selection

❋ Distribute copies of "My Millennium Time Line," pages 106–107. Have students preview the selection using the Preview Routine on page 39. Then, guide students as they apply the strategies they have learned for navigating text. Remind students to use the Reading Tools to read the time line.

❋ Before the second reading, use the lesson below to teach students about the selection's text structure: sequence.

Teaching the Text Structure: Sequence

Introduce Discuss the importance of identifying how text is structured. It alerts readers to how the text was written. This can help readers organize their thinking as they read. Tell students that historical articles are often written in chronological, or time, order.

Model You may wish to use the Think Aloud at right as you model how to determine the text structure of "My Millennium Time Line."

Guided Practice/Apply As students reread the selection, have them record the sequence of inventions in the time line on page 105. Then have students work in pairs to retell the information in their own words.

Think Aloud

Writers organize their writing in a way that helps us understand it. I see that "My Millennium Time Line" presents information in a sequence. Each label contains dates and information beginning in the year 1000 and continuing until the present. All the information on a time line appears in the order in which events happened, from the earliest time to the most recent.

Possible answers:

After you have completed the lesson, you may use the following questions to check students' comprehension:

1. What is the time period covered on this time line? *(the last millennium, or 1,000 years)*

2. What important household object was invented in the 1800s? *(telephone)*

3. When was a tool used for writing invented? What was it? *(The pencil was invented in the early 1500s.)*

4. How does the time line help you? *(Answers will vary.)*

Independent Practice: Writing

Have students write about their favorite invention on the time line.

W e b   L i n k s

www.grolier.com	Grolier (nonfiction books)
www.historyplace.com/index.html	The History Place
www.odci.gov/cia/publications/factbook	The World Book Factbook
www.historychannel.com	The History Channel
www.cbc4kids.ca/general/the-lab/histor	History of Inventions
www.invent.org/camp_invention	Camp Invention

What's the Order?

Place these inventions in order from first to last. Put a 1 beside the invention that happened first.

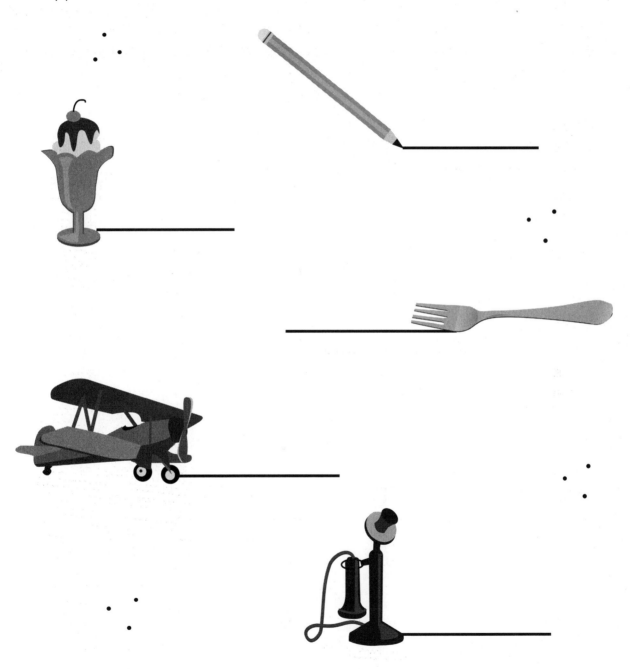

Extension Activity

Create a time line for the events of the past week.

My Millennium Time Line

Start Here! What happened during the last millennium, or one thousand years? Read the time line to find out when and where some exciting things got their start.

1000 **1100** **1200**

In the early 1000s the first **fireworks** are set off in China.

In the middle of the 1100s, people start playing **tennis** in France.

In the early 1200s, **chewing gum** becomes popular in Mexico.

1600 **1700** **1800**

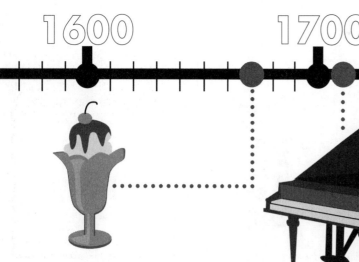

In the 1670s, **ice cream** is served in cafes in France.

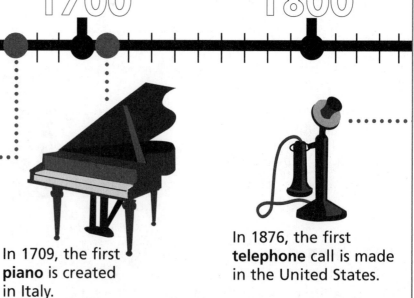

In 1709, the first **piano** is created in Italy.

In 1876, the first **telephone** call is made in the United States.

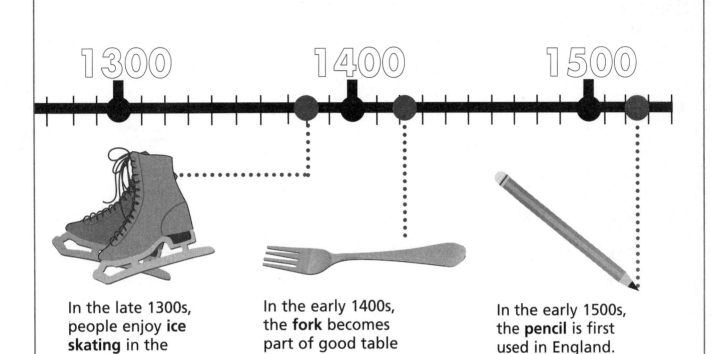

1300 **1400** **1500**

In the late 1300s, people enjoy **ice skating** in the Netherlands.

In the early 1400s, the **fork** becomes part of good table manners in Italy.

In the early 1500s, the **pencil** is first used in England.

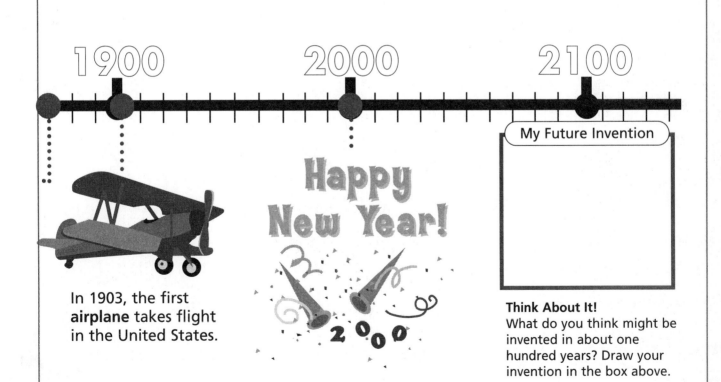

1900 **2000** **2100**

In 1903, the first **airplane** takes flight in the United States.

Happy New Year! 2000

My Future Invention

Think About It!
What do you think might be invented in about one hundred years? Draw your invention in the box above.

How to Read Primary Sources

What Are Primary Sources?

A primary source is an account of an event by someone who witnessed it. Letters, journals, photographs, interviews, newspaper accounts, and speeches are examples of primary sources. Sometimes a secondary source (e.g., a biography) includes primary source materials, such as photographs of and quotes by the person.

Why Are They Useful?

Primary sources are accounts of an event by someone who experienced it. Primary sources are usually very informative because they reveal the thoughts and feelings of people who were "on the scene." They provide snapshots in time of how people lived and what they thought about the current events. Primary sources help to personalize historical events for the reader.

Materials

▲ Reading Tools and Model Text, "Life on the Oregon Trail," pp. 110–111

▲ Transparency 10

▲ Bookmark, p. 150

Teaching the Lesson

Direct Instruction

✢ Distribute the Primary Source lesson, pages 110–111. Have students read the information about primary sources silently before discussing the model text together and using the Reading Tools.

✢ Then, use the **color transparency** to guide students as they read and use the Reading Tools.

✢ Use the Minilesson on page 109 to teach the text feature.

Teaching the Text Feature

Introduce Primary Sources Point out that primary sources are accounts of an event by someone who witnessed it. Letters, journals, photographs, interviews, newspaper accounts, and speeches are examples of primary sources. Many times, primary sources are embedded in secondary sources such as nonfiction books and biographies. To read a primary source embedded in a secondary source:

- Read the **main article**—the secondary source material. Sometimes the primary source material is embedded in the article. Other times, the primary source is in the side columns. Read this material after you finish reading the main material. Think about how the primary source adds to the information provided in the main article.

- Read the **primary source** material. Pay attention to who wrote it and when. Think about the time period. Notice the personal descriptions and reactions to the event. Ask yourself, "How does this information add to what I know about the topic?"

Model Use the Think Aloud at right to model how to read primary sources.

Guided Practice/Apply Have students read "Life on the Oregon Trail" on page 111 to experience firsthand accounts of traveling on the Oregon Trail in the mid-1800s. Make sure they can navigate the primary source diary entry within the larger article. Ask them to retell the information in their own words. You may also wish to ask the following:

1. When was the diary entry written? (*May 21, 1849*)

2. What important event was happening in the United States at that time? (*Many people were traveling to settle the West.*)

3. What was life like on the Oregon Trail? (*difficult, yet filled with many beautiful sights and interesting events*)

Together, the titles of the selection and of the insert at the bottom tell me that this article includes a diary entry from long ago, when people traveled in wagon trains across the country. An entry like this will help me understand what it was like for someone living during that time. Why did the person want to move to the West? What did the person feel about traveling in a wagon train? What was life really like for this person? These and other questions might be answered by the diary entry.

Comprehension QuickCheck

You may use the following questions to check students' comprehension:

1. What are primary sources? (*firsthand accounts of an event written by a person who witnessed it*)

2. Why are primary sources helpful? (*They tell the thoughts and feelings of people who experience an event.*)

3. What primary source material do you encounter every day? (*Answers will vary, but may include newspapers, diaries, letters, e-mails, and so on.*)

Primary Sources

You can learn about historical events in many ways. Some people who witnessed historical events kept records of them. These records are called primary sources. A **primary source** is an account of an event by someone who witnessed it. Letters, diaries, journals, photographs, interviews, newspaper accounts, and speeches are examples of primary sources. Primary sources tell the thoughts and feelings of people who were "on the scene."

Reading Tools

In this lesson, you will be reading an article about traveling west on the Oregon Trail during the mid-1800s. Included in the article is a diary entry from someone who traveled west. Use the Reading Tools below to help you read this kind of primary source.

◉ First, read the **title**. It tells you what the article is about.

◉ Then, **preview** the text to learn about the topic. Look for any primary source material, such as letters, photographs, quotes, and so on.

◉ Read the **main article**. Sometimes the primary source material is in the article. Other times, the primary source is in a side column. Read this material after you finish reading the main material.

◉ Read the **primary source** material. Pay attention to who wrote it and when. Think about the time period. Ask yourself, "How does this information add to what I know about the topic?"

Remember to use these Reading Tools when you read primary sources.

Life on the Oregon Trail

Life on the trail was oftentimes uncertain. Native Americans lived in many of the areas along the way. In fact, the Oregon Trail was not made by the pioneers. It went along a path that had been used years before by Native Americans. Sometimes Native Americans gave settlers advice about traveling along the trail. But sometimes the two groups fought with each other over the land. One way we know about the pioneers is from the **diaries** they kept. A diary is a written record of what someone has done or thought each day. Read the following words from a diary written by a 14-year-old girl named Sallie Hester. How was a day on the Oregon Trail different from one of your days?

Pioneers carved their names and dates of passage on big rocks to record their journey for others.

MANY VOICES
PRIMARY SOURCE

Diary written by Sallie Hester, May 21, 1849

Camped on the beautiful Blue River with plenty of wood and water and good grazing for our cattle. Our family all in good health. We had two deaths in our train within the past week of **cholera** (KAHL ur uh). When we camp at night, we form a **corral** with our wagons. We sleep in our wagons on feather beds. We live on bacon, ham, rice, dried fruits, molasses, packed butter, bread, coffee. Occasionally some of the men kill an antelope and then we have a feast; and sometimes we have fish on Sunday.

---

cholera: disease of the intestines
corral: fenced-in area for animals

Reading "The Oregon Trail"

M a t e r i a l s

▲ Student Text, "The Oregon Trail," pp. 116–117

▲ Graphic Organizer p. 115

Teaching the Lesson

Build Background

Distribute SmartChart Students will be reading an article about the Oregon Trail. Distribute copies of the SmartChart, page 152, or create one on chart paper. Use the routine on page 21. Through your questioning, guide the discussion to identify students' knowledge and/or misconceptions about the Oregon Trail or traveling west in the mid-1800s.

Share Information Share with students the following information prior to reading:

❈ In the mid-1800s, many people traveled west in search of gold, farmland, and new homes. The 2,000-mile trip took over five months.

❈ These people traveled by wagon train along well-established trails. Many of these trails were paths created and used for years by the Native Americans.

❈ A wagon train could have as many as 1,000 people and 3,000–4,000 animals, such as cows and horses. Large wagon trains stretched five miles and had over 100 wagons.

Related Words

pioneer . . . covered wagon

trail . . . covered wagon

communities . . . pioneer

territory . . . trail

Preteach Vocabulary

Preteach the following words from "The Oregon Trail" using the Vocabulary Routine on page 26. Or you may wish to use the Related Words chart shown at left. Have students tell how each pair of words is related. Encourage students to use the words in a sentence. The discussion will also give you an idea of how much knowledge students bring to the concepts they will be reading about.

Define each word. Be sure to point out unusual pronunciations, related words, and other aspects of the word.

- ✻ **pioneer** One of the first people to work or live in a new or unknown area

  Focus on pronunciation. Point out the open syllable at the beginning of the word: *pi-o-neer*. Remind students that an open syllable ends in a vowel and has a long vowel sound.

- ✻ **trail** A track or path for people to follow

  Focus on the related word *path*.

- ✻ **covered wagon** A large, wooden wagon with a canvas cover spread over metal hoops, used by pioneers crossing the United States during the mid-1800s

  Show students the illustration of a covered wagon included in the article.

- ✻ **territory** Any large area of land under the control of a state, nation, or ruler; can also refer to a part of the United States not admitted as a state. *The Oregon Territory was later divided and made into several states, such as Oregon, Washington, and Idaho.*

- ✻ **community** A group of people who live in the same area or who have something in common with each other. *Our community worked together to clean up the park.*

Read the Selection

- ✻ Distribute copies of "The Oregon Trail," pages 116–117. Have students preview the selection using the Preview Routine on page 39.
- ✻ Before the second reading, use the Minilesson below to teach students about the selection's text structure: problem and solution.

Teaching the Text Structure:
Problem and Solution

Introduce Discuss the importance of identifying how text is structured. It alerts readers to how the text was written. This can help them organize their thinking as they read. Tell students that they will focus on the structure of the opening deck for the article.

Model You may wish to use the Think Aloud at right as you model how to determine the text structure of "The Oregon Trail."

Guided Practice/Apply As students reread the selection, have them complete the primary source chart, page 115. Then have students work in pairs to retell the information in their own words.

Think Aloud

Writers organize their writing in a way that helps us understand it. I see that the article "The Oregon Trail" presents information about this famous path out west during the mid-1800s. I wonder why people wanted to travel west. The introduction at the top of the article explains that the East became crowded and there weren't enough jobs or farmland. This was a problem. It goes on to say that people went west to find better land and lead better lives. This is the solution to the problem. Therefore, I know that the text structure is problem and solution.

Possible answers:

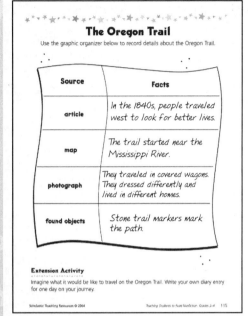

After you have completed the lesson, you may use the following questions to check students' comprehension:

1. When did people travel along the Oregon Trail? (*in the mid-1800s*)

2. What was the Oregon Trail? (*a kind of road that went west from Missouri to Oregon*)

3. Why did people want to move west? (*They wanted better lives and new homes.*)

4. How do we learn about the Oregon Trail today? (*books and primary sources such as diary entries, photographs, and artifacts from that time*)

5. How did the primary sources in the article add to your understanding of this time period? (*Answers will vary.*)

Independent Practice: Writing

Have students write a summary of the information they just read. Suggest that they use the graphic organizer they completed while reading to help them create their summaries. Have them include the following:

☀ a description of the Oregon Trail,

☀ what life was like on the Oregon Trail,

☀ why the Oregon Trail was important.

W e b L i n k s

www.isu.edu/~trinmich/Oregontrail.html	The Oregon Trail
www.californiawagontrail.com/index.htm	California National Historical Trail Wagon Trains
www.americaslibrary.gov	"America's Story" from the Library of Congress
www.pbs.org/lewisandclark/	Lewis and Clark on PBS
www.kidinfo.com/American-History/Pioneers.html	
	Trails West on Kid Info

The Oregon Trail

Use the graphic organizer below to record details about the Oregon Trail.

Source	Facts
article	
map	
photograph	
found objects	

Extension Activity

Imagine what it would be like to travel on the Oregon Trail. Write your own diary entry for one day on your journey.

THE OREGON TRAIL

BETTER LIVES AND NEW HOMES

In the 1840s, groups of people traveled west on the Oregon Trail. These people were looking for better lives and new homes. They became pioneers.

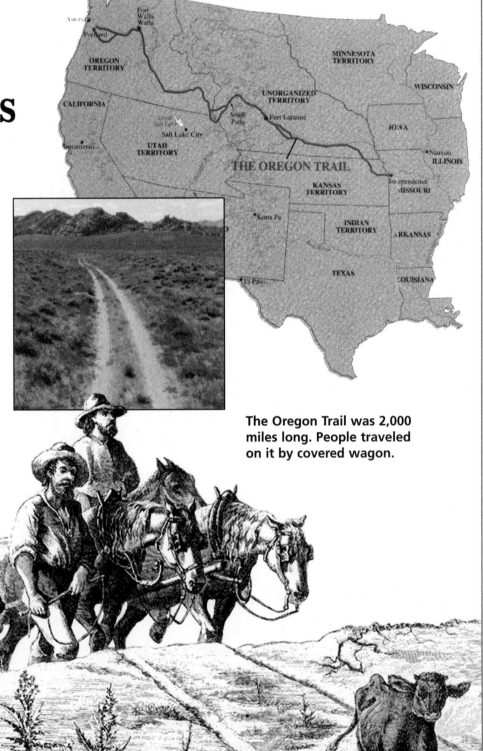

The Oregon Trail was 2,000 miles long. People traveled on it by covered wagon.

STARTING OUT FROM MISSOURI

Many people from different places came to Independence, Missouri. Independence is where the Oregon Trail begins. Sometimes 100 wagons traveled together.

> *"The prairie, oh, the broad, the beautiful, the bounding [hilly], rolling prairie! Imagine the ocean, when the waves are rolling mountains high, becoming solid and covered with beautiful green grass and you have some faint idea of it."*
>
> — Rebecca Ketchum, 1853

These people built new homes in the West.

THE END OF THE TRAIL

Out west, many people found land to farm. They cleared the land, planted crops, and built homes.

This trail marker was on the Oregon Trail.

How to Read Online News Articles

Spotlight

What Are Online News Articles?

An online news article is an article about a current event that is found on the Internet. To find an online article, readers can use a search engine. Through a search engine they can enter a keyword or subject and the search engine will direct them to links containing related information. Some search engines also have pre-designated areas to search. These areas contain Web pages and Web site listings that the managers of the search engine have collected. Once readers get to a Web page or site, they follow the directions provided to navigate it.

Why Are They Useful?

Online news articles present up-to-date information that anyone can access quickly and for free. Using a simple search engine, a reader can find all of the articles written on a particular topic, selecting those most appropriate for his or her reading needs. It is also easy to find a wide range of articles on any given topic faster than searching in a library.

Materials

▲ Reading Tools and Model Text, "A Day on Mars," pp. 120–121

▲ Transparency 11

▲ Bookmark, p. 150

Teaching the Lesson

Direct Instruction

✸ Distribute the Online News Article lesson, pages 120–121. Have students read the information about online sources silently before discussing the model text together and using the Reading Tools.

✸ Then, use the **color transparency** to guide students as they read and use the Reading Tools.

✸ Use the Minilesson on page 119 to teach the text feature.

Teaching the Text Feature

Introduce Online Sources Point out that online news articles contain information about current events and are found on the Internet. To read an online news article:

- Read the **title**. It tells you what the article is about.
- Look for a **date**. It tells you when the article was written. You can decide if the news is up-to-date.
- Click on the **picture** to make it bigger and then read the **caption**.
- Click on the **underlined words** in the article. More information about the word or about the topic will pop up on your screen. You might also see an encyclopedia article about related topics.
- Look for **buttons**. You can click on these buttons or words to get more information. Sometimes links to a dictionary are provided.

Model Use the Think Aloud at right to model how to read an online source.

Guided Practice/Apply Help students read "A Day on Mars" on page 121 to learn about the fourth planet in our solar system. Make sure they can navigate the online article and understand its unique features. Ask them to retell the information in their own words.

Think Aloud

As I read the online news article, I discover that I have a lot of information at my fingertips. After reading the main article, I can click on the photo to make it bigger, and I can click on underlined words to find out what they mean. I can also click on the link buttons to get more information about Mars. I can get stories, mini-movies, games, and even access to experts on Mars. It's like having five or six books on Mars in one.

Comprehension QuickCheck

You may use the following questions to check students' comprehension:

1. What are online articles? (*information about topics found on the Internet*)

2. What does this online article contain? (*facts, photos, links to other sites—all about Mars*)

3. How would you find more information about Mars? (*Answers will vary, but should include clicking on the web links provided and/or using a search engine.*)

4. If you had to tell a classmate about online articles, what would you say? (*Answers should reflect a clear understanding of online sources.*)

Online Articles

The Internet has opened up the world. Just turn on your computer and dial up a site. There, you can read an article about sports. You can find where movies are playing. You can even do research for school. **Online articles** offer up-to-date, minute-by-minute information.

These articles often have special features. You may be able to make a photograph larger. You may be able to find more facts about a topic. You may even be able to use an online dictionary.

Reading Tools

Use the tools below to help you read an online article.

◉ Read the **title**. It tells you what the article is about.

◉ Look for a **date**. If there is one, it tells you when the article was written.

◉ Click on the **picture** to look at it more clearly. Then read the **caption**.

◉ Click on the <u>underlined</u> or **highlighted words**. More information will pop up on your screen.

◉ Look for **buttons**, or **links**. You can click on these buttons or words to get more information. This article has links to photos, games, experts, and more.

Remember to use these Reading Tools when you read online articles.

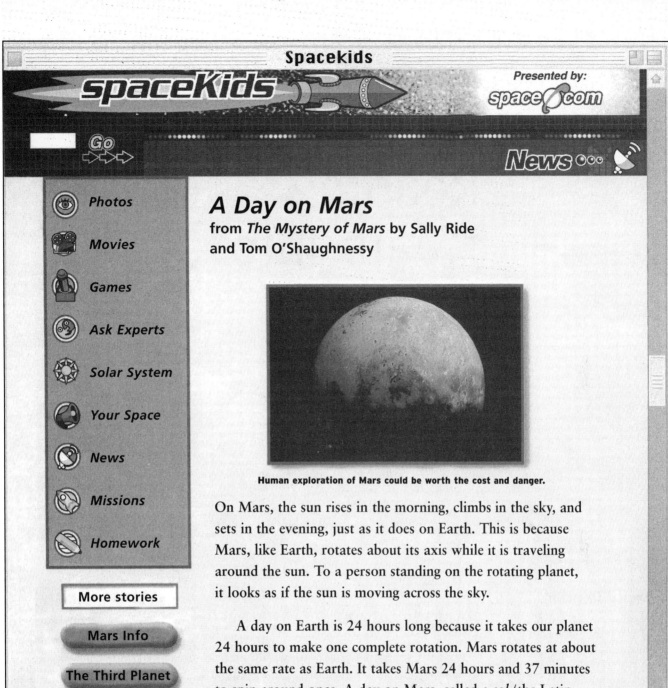

spaceKids

Presented by:
space com

Go

News ○○○

- Photos
- Movies
- Games
- Ask Experts
- Solar System
- Your Space
- News
- Missions
- Homework

More stories

Mars Info

The Third Planet

A Day on Mars
from *The Mystery of Mars* by Sally Ride and Tom O'Shaughnessy

Human exploration of Mars could be worth the cost and danger.

On Mars, the sun rises in the morning, climbs in the sky, and sets in the evening, just as it does on Earth. This is because Mars, like Earth, rotates about its axis while it is traveling around the sun. To a person standing on the rotating planet, it looks as if the sun is moving across the sky.

A day on Earth is 24 hours long because it takes our planet 24 hours to make one complete rotation. Mars rotates at about the same rate as Earth. It takes Mars 24 hours and 37 minutes to spin around once. A day on Mars, called a *sol* (the Latin word for "sun"), is 37 minutes longer than a day on Earth.

On some other planets, a "day" is very different. A day on Venus is very long—244 Earth days! This is because Venus rotates very slowly, only once every 244 days. A day on Jupiter is very short—only 10 hours long—because Jupiter rotates very quickly.

Reading "Mars Info"

- ▲ Student Text, "Mars Info," pp. 126–127
- ▲ Graphic Organizer p. 125

Teaching the Lesson
▲▲▲▲▲▲▲▲▲▲▲▲▲▲▲▲▲▲▲▲▲▲▲▲▲▲▲▲▲▲▲

Build Background

Distribute SmartChart Students will be reading more information about Mars in a related online article. Distribute copies of the SmartChart, page 152, or create one on chart paper. Use the routine on page 21. Through your questioning, guide the discussion to identify students' knowledge and/or misconceptions about Mars.

Share Information You may wish to share the following:

- ❀ Mars is the fourth planet from the sun in our solar system.
- ❀ Mars is the closest planet to Earth.
- ❀ Scientists have found evidence of water on Mars.

Preteach Vocabulary

Preteach the following words from "Mars Info" using the Vocabulary Routine on page 26. Or you may wish to use the drawing shown at left. Encourage students to share what they know about the words. The discussion will also give you an idea of how much knowledge students bring to the concepts they will be reading about.

Define each word. Be sure to point out unusual pronunciations, important sound-spelling relationships, related words, and other aspects of the word.

- ❀ **diameter** A straight line passing through the center of a circle, or the length of that line. *The diameter of that beach ball is 15 inches.* Help students pronounce the word.

- ❀ **rotate** To turn around and around like a wheel. *The Earth rotates, or spins around, completely once each day.* Point out the final *e* spelling pattern in the second syllable.

Labeled Drawing

Make a simple drawing of a planet on the chalkboard (a large circle). Use this drawing to illustrate each word. For example, when discussing diameter, draw a straight line through the center of the circle, from one side to the other.

diameter

rotate

orbit

craters

poles

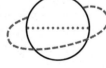

✺ **orbit** To travel around an object, such as a planet or the sun. *The planets orbit the sun.*

> Focus on the pronunciations of the smaller word parts: or-bit.

✺ **craters** A large hole in the ground caused by something such as a meteorite. *Many craters can be seen on the surface of the moon.*

> Focus on the related word, *holes*.

✺ **poles** The two points, or places, that are farthest away from the center of certain round objects; for example, the North Pole and the South Pole are the two points farthest away from the equator on Earth. *The poles on Earth are the coldest places.*

> Focus on multiple meanings—(1) a long, smooth piece of wood; (2) one of two opposite ends of a magnet; (3) "poles apart," as in two people who have opposite ideas.

Read the Selection

✺ Distribute copies of "Mars Info," pages 126–127. Have students preview the selection using the Preview Routine on page 39. Then, guide students as they apply the strategies they have learned for navigating text. Remind students to use the Reading Tools they learned to read the online article provided.

✺ Before the second reading, use the Minilesson below to teach students about the selection's text structure: description.

··· **M i n i l e s s o n** ·

Teaching the Text Structure: Description

Introduce Remind students that writers organize nonfiction in several ways called text structures. Knowing how a text is written can help readers organize their thinking as they read. Tell students that a science article often provides details about a topic.

Model You may wish to use the Think Aloud at right as you model how you figure out that description is the text structure of "Mars Info."

Guided Practice/Apply As students reread the selection, have them complete the Mars Fact Card, page 125. Then have students work in pairs to retell the information in their own words.

Think Aloud

Writers organize their writing in a way that helps us understand it. As I look at "Mars Info," I see a lot of details about this planet. For example, I read that this planet is covered in a red dust and is colder than Earth. This is a description of Mars. When I read articles like these—articles that are descriptions—I know that they will contain a lot of details. Therefore, I begin to collect and remember these details as I read.

Comprehension QuickCheck

Possible answers:

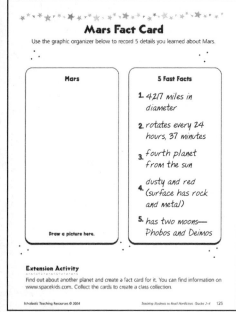

After you have completed the lesson, you may use the following questions to check students' comprehension:

1. How many moons does Mars have? (*two—Phobos and Deimos*)
2. Which planet is closer to the Sun—Mars or Earth? (*Earth*)
3. Why is Mars red in color? (*The dust on Mars is made of iron oxide, which looks red.*)
4. What special features do you see on the page? (*title, date, photograph, links for more information*)
5. What other information can you get about Mars? (*photos, movies, news, missions, etc.*)

Independent Practice: Writing

Have students e-mail to a friend, classmate, or family member three facts they learned about Mars.

Mars Fact Card

Use the graphic organizer below to record 5 details you learned about Mars.

Mars

Draw a picture here.

5 Fast Facts

1.

2.

3.

4.

5.

Extension Activity

Find out about another planet and create a fact card for it. You can find information on www.spacekids.com. Collect the cards to create a class collection.

spaceKids

Presented by:
space.com

Go

News ○○○

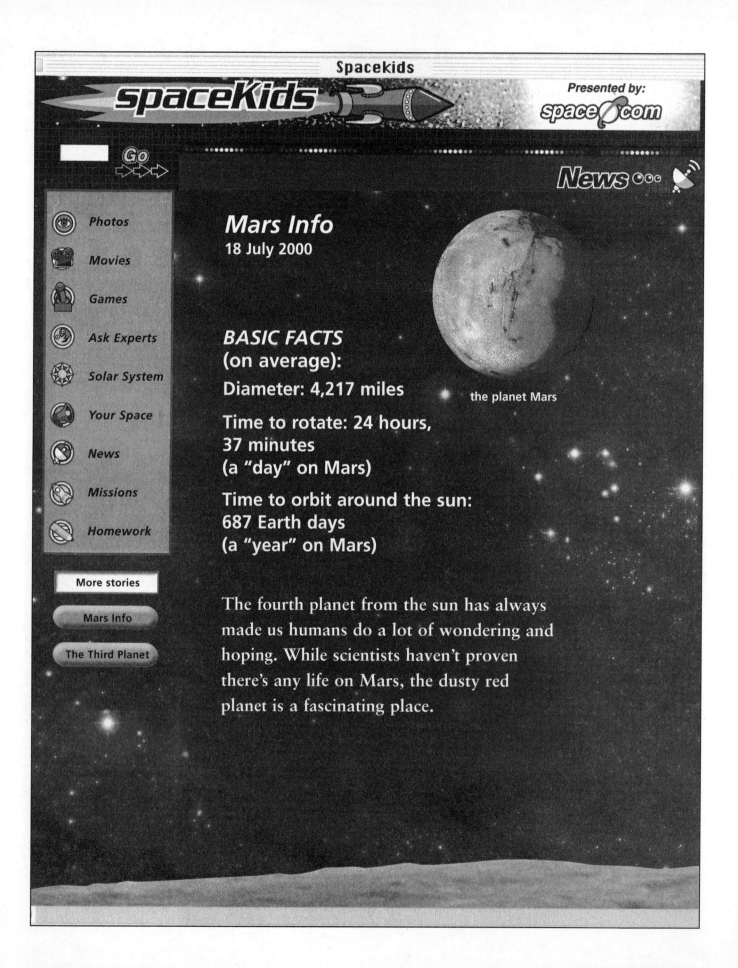

Mars Info
18 July 2000

the planet Mars

Navigation
- Photos
- Movies
- Games
- Ask Experts
- Solar System
- Your Space
- News
- Missions
- Homework

More stories

Mars Info

The Third Planet

BASIC FACTS
(on average):

Diameter: 4,217 miles

Time to rotate: 24 hours, 37 minutes
(a "day" on Mars)

Time to orbit around the sun: 687 Earth days
(a "year" on Mars)

The fourth planet from the sun has always made us humans do a lot of wondering and hoping. While scientists haven't proven there's any life on Mars, the dusty red planet is a fascinating place.

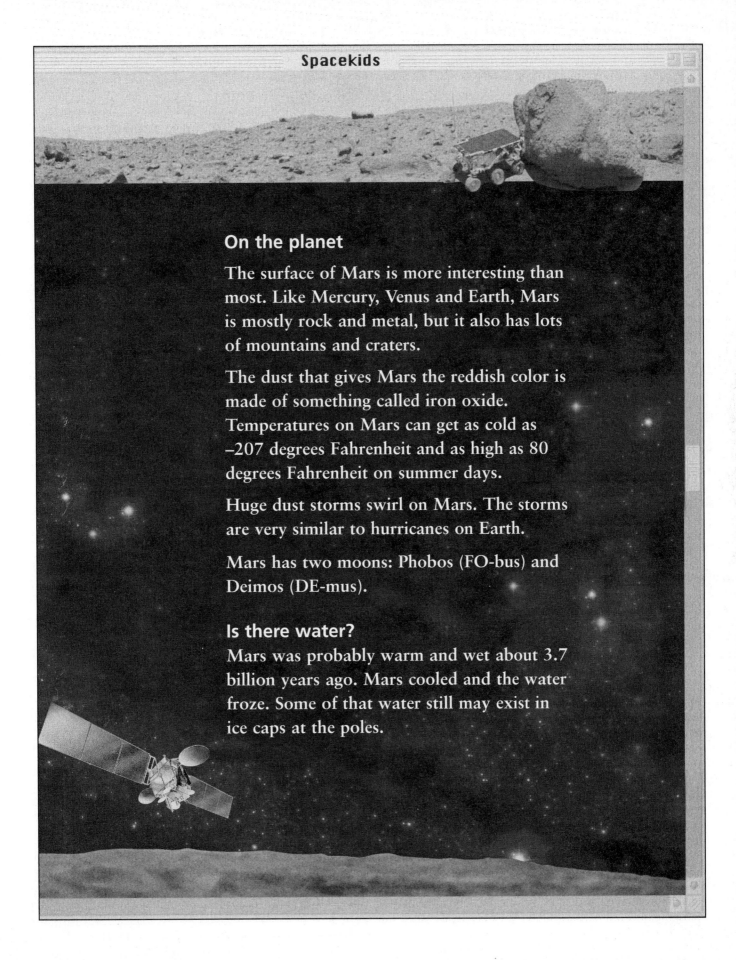

On the planet

The surface of Mars is more interesting than most. Like Mercury, Venus and Earth, Mars is mostly rock and metal, but it also has lots of mountains and craters.

The dust that gives Mars the reddish color is made of something called iron oxide. Temperatures on Mars can get as cold as –207 degrees Fahrenheit and as high as 80 degrees Fahrenheit on summer days.

Huge dust storms swirl on Mars. The storms are very similar to hurricanes on Earth.

Mars has two moons: Phobos (FO-bus) and Deimos (DE-mus).

Is there water?

Mars was probably warm and wet about 3.7 billion years ago. Mars cooled and the water froze. Some of that water still may exist in ice caps at the poles.

How to Read a Science Textbook

Materials

▲ Reading Tools
and Model Text,
"What Makes
Sound?,"
pp. 130–131

▲ Transparency 12

▲ Bookmark, p. 150

Spotlight

What Text Features Are in Science Textbooks?

Textbook reading can be very intimidating to some students for reasons that have been discussed in detail in a previous section of this book (see pages 7–9). It is important to make students aware that the features in their textbooks serve as aids to reading. These features are signposts that will help students navigate their way through the complex-looking pages of a science textbook.

Why Are They Useful?

Science textbooks contain many reader-friendly features that help guide students through the material so that they will better comprehend and remember what they are reading. Use examples from the students' science textbook as you discuss the following features:

- The **chapter title** tells the reader what the topic is.

- **Headings** of sections tell the reader what he or she will read about in that particular part of the chapter.

- Both the title and the headings give the reader a good idea of the **main ideas** that will be covered. This information allows students to anticipate what the lesson will be about. Students should develop the habit of verbalizing this to themselves by saying, **"This lesson will be about. . . ."**

- Print features are additional alert signals. **Boldfaced words** highlight important vocabulary to remember. A difficult word may be followed by its **pronunciation**.

- **Graphic aids** are especially useful and informative. They clarify the text and help the reader visualize the concepts. Photographs are interesting to look at, and they bring the subject to life. Diagrams help make complex processes clearer. Ask students to imagine their textbook pages without the graphic aids. How dull the book would look, and how much harder it would be to understand the information!

Teaching the Lesson

Direct Instruction

❈ Distribute the Science Textbook lesson, pages 130-131. Have students read the information about reading science textbooks silently before discussing the model text together and using the Reading Tools.

❈ Then display the **color transparency** and use it to guide students as they read and use the Reading Tools.

❈ Use the Minilesson below to model how you approach a page in a science textbook.

Think Aloud

When I finish reading, I look at the photo and the diagrams. They illustrate what I read. I read the labels to learn what the diagrams are showing. They are close-ups of the vocal cords which, of course, we can't see. The label on one diagram says that the vocal cords are closed. I know from my reading that that's because the girl is using her voice. The label on the other diagram says that the vocal cords are open. That's because the girl is not using her voice.

The lines from the diagram to the girls show where the vocal cords are located in the body—in a person's throat.

The drawings help me get a clear picture of what I read about vocal cords.

Teaching the Text Feature

Introduce Science Textbook Features Explain to students that photographs and diagrams illustrate the information in the text. They help readers form clear pictures in their minds of what they are reading.

Point out the two diagrams (drawings). They show close-ups of the vocal cords—something that can't be seen in the photo. The lines leading from each drawing to one of the girls show where the vocal cords are located inside the body. Stress that it is important to read the labels. They tell readers what they're looking at.

Model Use the Think Aloud at right to model how you use the graphic aids.

Guided Practice/Apply Have students read aloud the section of the text that describes what is pictured in the photograph and the diagram. Ask them to explain how the diagram helped them visualize what they read.

Comprehension QuickCheck

After you have completed the lesson, you may wish to ask the following:

1. What do your vocal cords look like when you are talking? (*closed*) when you are just listening? (*open*)

2. What is another word for vibrations? (*movements*)

3. Why is a diagram included in the lesson? (*to illustrate the information*)

Science Textbook Features

Some of the information you read in school comes from your textbooks. Take a look at a **science textbook**.

You can see that it has more than just text in it. There are many features, too. You may see headings, diagrams, photos with captions, maps, and charts. Maybe you're thinking, "What is all this stuff? What should I look at first?"

All the features are there to help you. But first you must know how to use them. Once you do, you'll better understand what you read—and you'll remember it better, too.

Reading Tools

Use the tools to help you read a science lesson.

◉ Read the **title**. It tells you what the lesson is about.

◉ Read any **headings**. They tell you the main ideas.

◉ Say to yourself, **"This lesson will be about . . . ."**

◉ Pay special attention to the **boldfaced words**. They are important vocabulary words to remember.

◉ Study the **photos** carefully. They will help you picture the information in the text.

◉ Read the **captions** and **labels**. They explain the photo. Sometimes they give new information, too.

Remember to use these Reading Tools when you read your science textbook.

What Makes Sound?

Whoosh! Bang! Clatter. Mmmm . . . What could have made those sounds? Even sounds that are very different are all alike in one important way. All sounds are made by a certain kind of motion. What kind of motion makes sound?

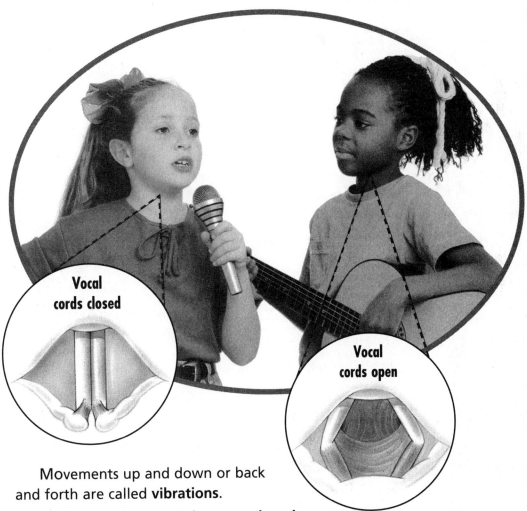

Vocal cords closed

Vocal cords open

Movements up and down or back and forth are called **vibrations**.

Inside your throat you have **vocal cords**. They're like two leathery flaps. Normally they have a space between them so you can breathe. But when you use your voice, your vocal cords move close together. Then air coming up from your lungs moves between them. The air makes your vocal cords **vibrate**.

Reading "Sounds All Around"

Materials

▲ Student Text, "Sounds All Around," pp. 136–137

▲ Graphic Organizer p. 135

Teaching the Lesson

Build Background

Distribute SmartChart Tell students that they will read a section from a science textbook. It's about how people and animals hear. Distribute copies of the SmartChart, page 152. Ask students what they know about how we hear. What they say will inform you of gaps or misconceptions in their prior knowledge.

Share Information Based on your students' prior knowledge, share with them the background knowledge they will need to comprehend "Sounds All Around."

※ Sound waves travel into your ear and make your eardrum vibrate.

※ Your eardrum makes the tiny bones in your middle ear vibrate. The bones send the vibrations to your inner ear.

※ Your inner ear turns the vibrations into a signal that your brain can understand.

Preteach Vocabulary

Preteach the following words from "Sounds All Around" using the Vocabulary Routine on page 26. Or you may wish to use the Related Words activity at left.

Define each word and provide an example sentence. Also point out any unusual pronunciations, synonyms, antonyms, and related words. As you read, help students define *membrane* by using the context clues in the text.

※ **vibrations** Fast movements from side to side.
Connect to the verb *vibrate*, to move back and forth very fast.
A drum vibrates when you hit it.

Related Words

Explain to students that both pairs of words in each sentence are related. For example, they may be opposites or have almost the same meaning. Tell students to read the first word pair and figure out how they are related. Then choose the vocabulary word that best completes the second pair.

▲ **Outside** is to **outer** as **inside** is to _____.

▲ **Move** is to **movements** as **vibrate** is to _____.

▲ **Music** is to **musical** as **voice** is to _____.

▲ **Outside** is to **inside** as **outer** is to _____.

▲ **Voice** is to **vocal** as **sign** is to _____.

* **signal** A sign or message. *The bell was a signal that school was over for the day.*

* **inner** Farther inside. *You can't see the inner ear because it's inside the head.*

    Point out the related word *inside*. Also, explain that the opposite of *inner* is *outer*, as in *outer ear*.

* **vocal** Having to do with the voice. *Vocal music is music that is sung.*

Read the Selection

* Distribute copies of "Sounds All Around," pages 136–137. Remind students to use the Reading Tools they learned for how to read a science textbook. Also, point out the two diagrams with insets and review how they should be read.

* Before the second reading, use the Minilesson to teach students about the selection's text structure: cause and effect.

Teaching the Text Structure:
Cause and Effect

Introduce Remind students that a writer organizes nonfiction in several ways called text structures. Writers may:

* **compare and contrast** two people, places, or things;
* **describe** someone or something;
* tell the **sequence**, or order, in which something happens;
* tell about a **problem and its solution**; or
* explain the **cause and effect** of something.

Explain to students that knowing how a text is organized helps readers better understand and remember the information.

Model Use the Think Aloud at right as you model how you figured out that the text structure of "Sounds All Around" is cause and effect.

Guided Practice/Apply As students reread the selection, have them complete the graphic organizer for cause and effect, page 135. Then have students work in pairs to retell the information in their own words.

Think Aloud

Writers organize their writing in a way that helps us understand it. So when I read, I look for clues that tell me how the writing is organized.

The second paragraph explains what happens when something like a cymbal vibrates. It's causes the air around it to move. It creates a sound wave. That's the effect.

The sound wave travels to your ear and causes the air inside your ears to move. The effect is that you hear the cymbal. I see that the writer is describing cause and effect.

As I continue to read about how animals' ears work, I look for more causes and effects.

Possible answers:

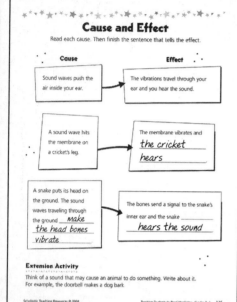

After you have completed the lesson, you may use the following questions to check students' comprehension.

1. What travels through the air when something vibrates? (*sound waves*)

2. What are sound waves traveling through when you feel the beat of music vibrating in the floor? (*the wood of the floor*)

3. Can sound waves travel through water? How do you know? (*Yes; Fish can hear.*)

4. Which animal do you think has the best hearing: a cricket, a fox, or a snake? Why? (*Fox; Students should be able to explain their answer.*)

5. How do the diagrams help you understand the way snakes and crickets hear? (*Answers will vary.*)

Independent Practice: Writing

Have students write two or three sentences about how a snake, a fox, or a cricket hears.

www.exploratorium.com The Exploratorium

www.grolier.com Grolier

134

Cause and Effect

Read each cause. Then finish the sentence that tells the effect.

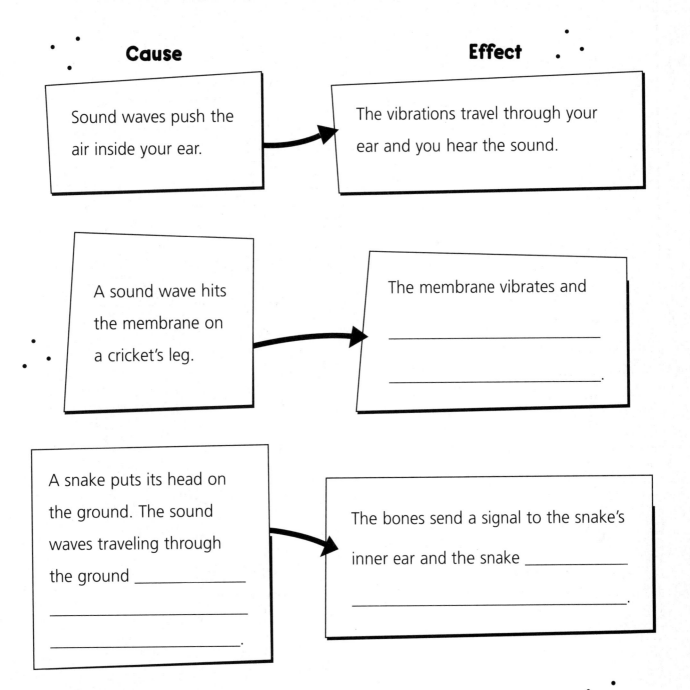

Cause

Effect

Sound waves push the air inside your ear.

The vibrations travel through your ear and you hear the sound.

A sound wave hits the membrane on a cricket's leg.

The membrane vibrates and _____ _____.

A snake puts its head on the ground. The sound waves traveling through the ground _____ _____ _____.

The bones send a signal to the snake's inner ear and the snake _____ _____.

Extension Activity

Think of a sound that may cause an animal to do something. Write about it. For example, the doorbell makes a dog bark.

Sounds All Around

How Vibrations Reach Your Ears

A doorbell rings. The people who are at home hear it. What's between the doorbell and the people who hear it? How do vibrations get to your ears where you hear them as sound?

When something vibrates—like a cymbal—it pushes the air around it. That air pushes more air and that air pushes more air until the air inside your ear gets pushed, too. That motion between the cymbal and your ear is a **sound wave**.

How do the vibrations from this crashing cymbal reach your ears?

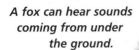

A fox can hear sounds coming from under the ground.

What Sound Waves Travel Through

Sound waves travel through air when you listen to a CD player from across a room. If the music's loud enough, you can feel the beat vibrating in the floor. What are the CD's sound waves traveling through?

Sound waves must travel through matter like air, wood, or water to reach you. Like you, fish can hear sounds underwater, too. Some fish, such as catfish, send sounds to one another. How do you think fish called grunts and croakers get their names?

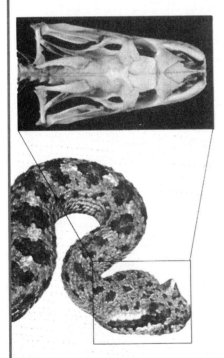

How Other Animals' Ears Work

Some animals have ears that can do things human ears can't. A fox's large ears turn to hear sounds coming from any direction.

Snakes don't have ears you can see. But a snake can hear by putting its head on the ground. Sound waves traveling through the ground make the bones in the snake's head vibrate. The bones send the signal to the snake's inner ear.

You might think that a cricket has no ears—unless you know where to look.

A snake has no outer ears but can hear!

A cricket hears with a vibrating membrane—a thin piece of skin—on each front leg.

How to Read a Social Studies Textbook

Materials

▲ Reading Tools and Model Text, "Iroquois Communities," pp. 140–141

▲ Transparency 13

▲ Bookmark, p. 150

Spotlight

What Text Features Are in Social Studies Textbooks?

Textbook reading can be confusing and even intimidating to many students for reasons that have been discussed in detail in Section 1 of this book (see pages 7–9). Our job is to make students aware of how the features in textbooks can help them read and understand the material. It may be slow going at first; students will need a great deal of guidance. But with repeated exposure and practice, students will begin to use these text features and become increasingly competent at applying them.

Why Are They Useful?

Textbooks include many features to make them "student friendly."
- The **chapter title** tells the reader what the topic is.
- The **headings** alert the reader to the main ideas in the text.
- The **graphic aids** illustrate information in the text and/or provide additional facts.

Teaching the Lesson

Direct Instruction

❋ Reading a social studies textbook is similar to reading a science textbook (see Lesson 17). Students will probably recognize that both kinds of textbooks have many features in common. You may want to acknowledge once again that textbooks can look daunting because

1. their pages often have several different type sizes, and
2. there's a lot of "stuff" on the page in addition to the main reading.

❋ Distribute the Social Studies lesson, pages 140–141. Have students read the information about social studies textbooks silently before discussing the model text together and using the Reading Tools.

❋ Display the **color transparency** and use it to guide students as they read the Reading Tools and apply them to the Model Text.

❋ Use the Minilesson below to teach students how to use the primary sources in the text.

Teaching the Text Feature

Introduce Social Studies Textbook Features Explain to students that social studies textbooks often make use of primary sources, which give us direct information about how people lived in the past. **Artifacts** are one primary source; they are objects that were made by people in the past. Some examples of artifacts are

- everyday tools and utensils, such as plows and cooking vessels
- toys
- clothing
- photographs, and
- works of art, such as statues.

Model Use the Think Aloud at right to model how to use primary sources.

Guided Practice/Apply After students read "Iroquois Communities," have them discuss additional information that they learned from the primary sources. For example, there was no door on the longhouse, the opening was covered with animal skins, and the building had to be tightly made to keep out the snow.

Think Aloud

One of the ways we learn about the past is through primary sources. A primary source may be a person. It may also be an object, called an artifact, that can give us information about the way people lived in the past.

In "Iroquois Communities," I see two artifacts. One is a clay jar that was used for storage. It shows me that in the 1600s the Iroquois did not have plastic or glass jars and containers, so they used natural materials to make what they needed. The photograph of the longhouse model shows me that the dwellings were made of branches and bark. I can also see why they were called longhouses!

Comprehension QuickCheck

You may use the following questions to check students' comprehension.

1. Why are artifacts and other primary sources helpful? (*They are real objects that give us information about how people lived in the past.*)

2. Why did the five groups of Iroquois join together? (*to help each other*)

3. What are some of the ways in which the groups may have helped each other? (*They may have: protected each other against enemies; shared with each other when food was scarce; exchanged goods; helped each other in times of illness or natural disasters.*)

Social Studies Textbook Features

Reading a **social studies textbook** is like reading a science textbook. The topics are not the same, of course. But both kinds of textbooks have many features to help you understand what you are reading.

In your social studies textbook, you may see maps, photos with captions, illustrations, and graphs. You may also see headings, boldfaced words, and pronunciations. These features are tools—reading tools. If you know how to use them, they will help you better understand and remember what you read.

Reading Tools

Use the tools below to help you read "Iroquois Communities."

◉ Read the **title**. It tells you what the lesson is about.

◉ Then **preview** the text to learn about the topic.

◉ Read the **introduction** and the **headings**.

◉ Look at the **photos**.

◉ Say to yourself, **"This lesson will be about . . . ."**

◉ Now read the text. Try to remember the **boldfaced words**. They are important vocabulary words.

◉ Use the **pronunciations**.

◉ Study the **primary sources**. Think about what the illustrations, captions, and quotations tell you about the past.

Remember to use these Reading Tools when you read your social studies textbook.

IROQUOIS COMMUNITIES

More than 400 years ago, five groups of Native Americans joined together. They thought this would make them stronger. They formed the Iroquois Confederation.

JOINING TOGETHER

The **Iroquois** (EAR-uh-qwoy) belonged to different groups that spoke the same language. Two great Iroquois leaders decided the groups should join together. They thought the groups could help each other.

▲ Deganawida and Hiawatha were two great Iroquois leaders.

MAKING DECISIONS

Each of the five Iroquois groups made some of its own decisions. Each of the five groups also chose members to be part of the Grand Council. The Grand Council made decisions for the whole Iroquois community.

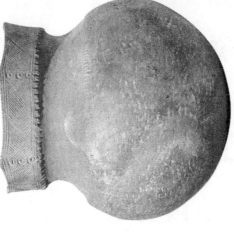

▲ The Iroquois stored their food in clay pots like this one.

"The doors of the lodges are of sheets of bark with neither key nor lock.... During all the centuries before our arrival, they lived in great security and without much distrust of each other."

—from the diary of a French explorer in 1724

WORKING TOGETHER

The five Iroquois groups were the Mohawk, Cayuga, Oneida, Seneca, and the Onondaga. They worked together to build special houses called **longhouses**. They built them out of wood and tree bark.

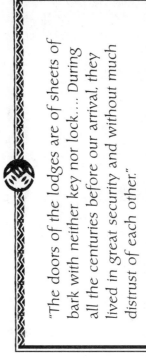

▲ This is a model of a traditional longhouse. Many families lived together. It was built for 80 to 120 people.

Reading "The Great Migration"

Materials

▲ Student Text, "The Great Migration," pp. 146–147

▲ Graphic Organizer p. 145

Teaching the Lesson

Build Background

Distribute SmartChart Students will be reading about the Great Migration, from a chapter in a social studies textbook. Distribute copies of the SmartChart, page 152, or create one on chart paper. Use the routine on page 21. Through your questioning, guide the discussion to identify students' knowledge and/or misconceptions about the Great Migration.

Share Information Based on students' prior knowledge, share any or all the following information prior to reading:

❊ Since colonial times, most African Americans had not been a free people. They had been living as slaves, forced to work for their owners. They were not allowed to learn to read or write.

❊ From 1861 to 1865, the northern states and the southern states were at war against each other. This was called the Civil War. Abraham Lincoln was president at this time.

❊ People in the South wanted to be separate from the North. They wanted to start their own country. People in the North wanted both parts of the U.S. to stay together as one country. President Lincoln also wanted to end slavery.

❊ The Civil War ended in 1865. The country remained together as one. Slavery was over, and African Americans were free.

Preteach Vocabulary

Preteach the following words from "The Great Migration" using the Vocabulary Routine on page 26. Or you may wish to use the Word Pairs chart shown at left. The discussion will also give you an idea of how much knowledge students bring to the concepts they will be reading about. Encourage students to use each word in a sentence.

Word Pairs

1. Draw the chart on the board.
2. Go over the meaning of each word.
3. Ask students to think about how each word pair is related.
4. Complete the chart.
5. Discuss.

	Same meaning	Opposite meaning	Go Together. Why?
migrate move	(✔)		
communities neighborhoods	(✔)		
products factories			(Products are made in factories.)
fairly unfairly		(✔)	
opportunities jobs			(People want the opportunity to get a good job.)
difficult easy		(✔)	

Define each word. As you read, help students define *factories* by using the context clues in the text.

❋ **migrate** To move from one part of a country to another. *Many families migrated from the South to the North.*
  Discuss the related word *migration*, as in The Great Migration. Point out that a migration is the movement of people from one part of a country to another.

❋ **communities** A group of people who live or work together in the same place. *I have a lot of friends in my community.*
  Discuss the related word *neighborhood*.

❋ **difficult** Hard; not easy. *It was difficult to lift the heavy box of books.* Point out that the opposite of *difficult* is *easy.*

❋ **factories** Buildings where people use machines to make things. *Cars and trucks are made in factories.*

❋ **opportunities** Good chances to do something. *There are many opportunities to play different sports in my school.*

Read the Selection

❋ Distribute copies of "The Great Migration," pages 146–147. Have students preview the selection using the Preview Routine on page 39.

❋ Before the second reading, use the Minilesson below to teach students about the selection's text structure: cause and effect.

Teaching the Text Structure:
Cause and Effect

Introduce Remind students that a writer organizes nonfiction in several ways called text structures. Writers may:

- **compare and contrast** two people, places, or things;
- **describe** someone or something;
- tell the **sequence**, or order, in which something happens;
- tell about a **problem and its solution**; or
- explain the **cause and effect** of something.

Explain to students that knowing how a text is organized helps readers better understand and remember the information.

Model Use the Think Aloud at right as you model how to identify that the text structure of "The Great Migration" is cause and effect.

Guided Practice/Apply As students reread the selection, have them complete the graphic organizer for cause and effect, page 145.

Think Aloud

As you know, writers organize their writing in a way that helps us better understand it. So when I read, I look for clues that tell me how the writing is organized.

In the section called "Difficult Lives," the writer explains that life was very hard for African Americans in the South after the Civil War. Then the writer tells us that many African Americans moved to cities in the north. Poor jobs and few chances for a good education caused African Americans to move.

Many African Americans who moved to the North found jobs. Some started their own businesses. The effect was that their lives improved. I see that the writer is describing cause and effect.

As I read about Jacob Lawrence, I will continue to look for causes and effects.

143

Comprehension QuickCheck

Possible answers:

After you have completed the lesson, you may use the following questions to check students' comprehension:

1. What caused The Great Migration? (*People had hard lives in the South after the Civil War. They moved North to find better jobs, housing, and a better education.*)

2. Why was their move called *The Great Migration*? (*because so many people moved North*)

3. What primary sources are in the selection? (*part of a letter written by a woman who migrated north and a painting by an African American artist*)

4. What did you learn from the primary sources in the selection? (*The letter shows us how happy a woman who migrated was in her new city. Lawrence's painting shows us one scene from life in the North after the Great Migration.*)

5. How do you pronounce I-l-l-i-n-o-i-s? (*ill-uh-NOY*)

Independent Practice: Writing

Have students write two short paragraphs. In the first paragraph, they should tell why many African Americans migrated to the North after the Civil War. In the second, they should tell about the kind of lives they hoped to have in the North.

Web Links

teacher.scholastic.com/fieldtrp/socstu.htm	Scholastic
www.americaslibrary.gov	"America's Story" from the Library of Congress
www.nmai.si.edu	National Museum of the American Indian
www.s9.com/biography	Biographical Dictionary
americanhistory.si.edu	National Museum of American History

The Great Migration

In the chart below, write the causes and effects of the Great Migration.

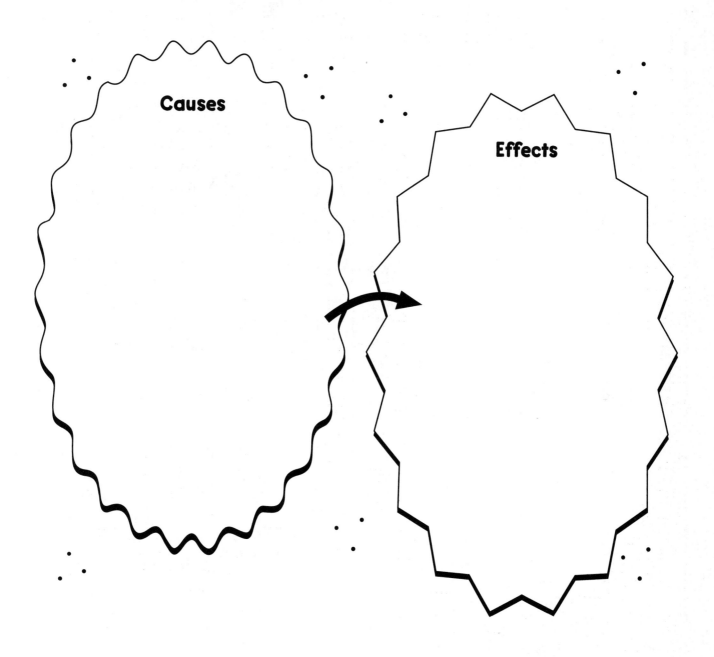

Causes

Effects

Extension Activity

Imagine that you were in the Great Migration. Write a letter to a friend back home telling where you were living, what kind of work you were doing, and how you felt about your new life.

THE GREAT MIGRATION

In the early 1900s, many African Americans migrated, or moved, from the South to the North. They hoped to find a better way of life in the cities of the North.

DIFFICULT LIVES

Although they were free, life was still hard for African Americans living in the South after the Civil War. There were very few chances for good jobs or education. African Americans were still not treated fairly.

In the early 1900s, African Americans heard there were good jobs and better opportunities in northern cities like Chicago, Detroit, New York, and Philadelphia. Thousands of people moved north hoping for a better life. The Great Migration began.

▲
Thousands of African Americans made the journey to northern cities to look for better jobs.

◄
Many African Americans in the South lived in rural communities where they were not treated fairly.

STARTING OVER

Starting a new life in the North was exciting for many African Americans. One woman wrote a letter to her family about her life in Chicago, Illinois (il-uh-NOY). She said, "I am well and thankful to be in a city. . . . The people are rushing here by the thousands. The houses are so pretty, we have a nice place. Hurry up and come to Chicago. It is wonderful. . . ."

Communities grew in the North. There were more opportunities to find jobs. People worked in iron and steel mills. Some made buildings. Many worked in factories where they made products like bricks and glass. Others worked on railroads. Their lives were improving. As their communities grew, some people started their own businesses. Many people were happy with their decision to migrate to the North.

In addition to painting the Great Migration, Jacob Lawrence also painted many scenes of African American life, like this one. ▶

Jacob Lawrence
▼

PAINTING THE GREAT MIGRATION

As a young boy, Jacob Lawrence became interested in painting. He knew he wanted to be an artist. About 1917, his parents migrated north to Philadelphia. Years later, Jacob Lawrence made a series of paintings about the Great Migration.

Bookmarks

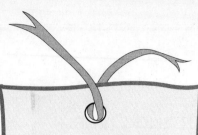

How to Read Nonfiction Text

✔ Read the **title**.

✔ Read the **introduction** and the **headings**.

✔ **Predict** what the article will be about.

✔ Remember the **boldfaced words**.

✔ Use the **pronunciations**.

✔ Study the **special features**.

Lesson 1

How to Read an Encyclopedia Article

✔ First, read the **title**.

✔ Next, find the **headings**.

✔ Finally, look at the **pictures**.

Lesson 3

How to Read a Diagram

✔ First, read the **title** and **introduction**.

✔ Look at the **labels**.

✔ Follow the **arrows**.

✔ Finally, look for **pronunciations**.

Lesson 5

How to Read a Map

- ✔ Read the map **title**.
- ✔ Find the **symbols**.
- ✔ Look at the map **key**.
- ✔ Read the **labels** on the map.
- ✔ Find the **compass rose**.

Lesson 7

How to Read a Flow Chart

- ✔ Read the **title**.
- ✔ Follow the **numbers** in order.
- ✔ Read each **label** and study each **picture**.
- ✔ Read each **explanation**.
- ✔ Follow the **arrows**.
- ✔ Remember the **boldfaced words**.
- ✔ Use the **pronunciations**.

Lesson 9

How to Read a Magazine Article

- ✔ Read the **headline** and **headings**.
- ✔ Say to yourself, **"This article will be about...."**
- ✔ Use the **pronunciations**.
- ✔ Remember the **boldfaced words**.
- ✔ Study the **photos** and **graphs** or **diagrams**.
- ✔ Read the **captions**.

Lesson 11

How to Read Time Lines

- ✔ First, read the **title**.
- ✔ Then, read the **introduction**.
- ✔ Find the starting and ending **dates**.
- ✔ Read the **labels** for each date.

Lesson 13

How to Read Primary Sources

✔ First, read the **title**

✔ **Preview** the text to learn about the topic.

✔ Read the **main article**.

✔ Read the **primary source** material. Ask yourself, "How does this information add to what I know about the topic?"

Lesson 15

How to Read Online News Articles

✔ Read the **title**.

✔ Look for a **date**.

✔ Click on the **picture** to make it bigger. Then read the **caption**.

✔ Click on the **underlined** or **highlighted words** for more information.

✔ Look for **buttons**, or **links**.

Lesson 17

How to Read a Science Textbook

✔ Read the **title** of the lesson or chapter.

✔ Read the **headings**.

✔ Say to yourself, **"This lesson will be about…."**

✔ Remember the **boldfaced words**.

✔ Study the **photos** and other **graphic aids**.

✔ Read the **captions** and **labels**.

Lesson 19

How to Read a Social Studies Textbook

✔ Read the **title** of the lesson.

✔ **Preview** the lesson by reading the **introduction** and **headings**.

✔ Say to yourself, **"This lesson will be about…."**

✔ Remember the **boldfaced words**.

✔ Use the **pronunciations**.

✔ Study the **primary sources**.

Bibliography

Alvermann, Donna E. and Stephen F. Phelps. 1998. *Content Reading and Literacy: Succeeding in Today's Diverse Classrooms.* Second Edition. Needham Heights, MA: Allyn & Bacon.

Carnine, Douglas W., Jerry Silbert, Edward J. Kameenui. 1997. *Direct Instruction Reading.* Third Edition. Upper Saddle River, NJ: Prentice-Hall.

Cooper, J. David. 1993. Literacy: *Helping Children Construct Meaning.* Second Edition. Boston: Houghton Mifflin Company.

CORE (Consortium on Reading Excellence). 1999. Novato, CA: Arena Press.

Duke, Nell K. and V. Susan Bennett-Armisted. 2003. *Reading and Writing Informational Text in the Primary Grades.* New York: Scholastic Inc.

Lapp, Diane, James Flood, and Nancy Farnan. 1996. *Content Area Reading and Learning: Instructional Strategies.* Second Edition. Needham Heights, MA: Allyn & Bacon.

Vacca, Richard T. and Jo Anne L. Vacca. 1999. *Content Area Reading: Literacy and Learning Across the Curriculum.* Sixth Edition. New York: Addison-Wesley Educational Publishers Inc.

Web Links

www.scholastic.com	Scholastic
teacher.scholastic.com/newszone/index.asp	Scholastic (current events)
www.grolier.com	Grolier (nonfiction books)
www.sln.org	The Science Learning Network
www.historyplace.com/index.html	The History Place
www.s9.com/biography	Biographical Dictionary
www.graphic.org	Graphic Organizers
www.educationplanet.com	Education Planet
www.homeworkcentral.com	Homework Central
www.mcn.edu/sitesonline.htm	The Museum Guide
www.edhelper.com	EdHelper.com (lesson plans)
www.ed.gov/free	FREE (Federal Resources for Educational Excellence)
www.pbs.org/teachersource	PBS
school.discovery.com/schoolhome.html	Discovery Channel School
www.odci.gov/cia/publications/factbook	The World Book Factbook
www.mcrel.org/whelmers	McRel Science Activities

Related Internet Reference Books

Homework on the Internet by Marianne J. Dyson (Scholastic, 2000)

1001 Best Websites for Educators by Timothy Hopkins (Teacher Created Materials, 2001)

Internet Made Easy: 10 Quick & Fun Internet Field Trips by Deirdre Kelly (Scholastic, 2000)

SmartChart

B Background	K What We Know	W What We Want to Know	L What We Learned

Teaching Students to Read Nonfiction, Grades 2–4

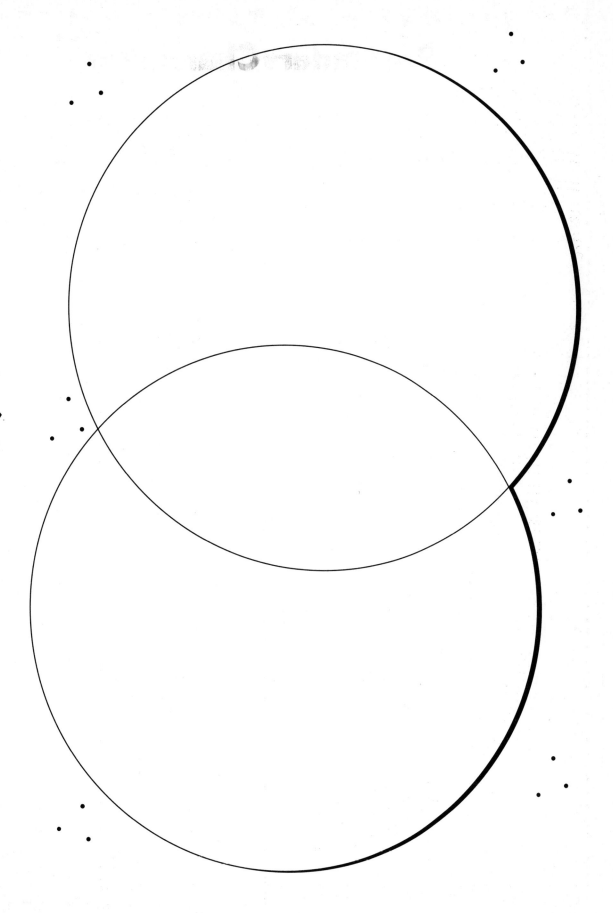

Venn Diagram

Prereading Organizer

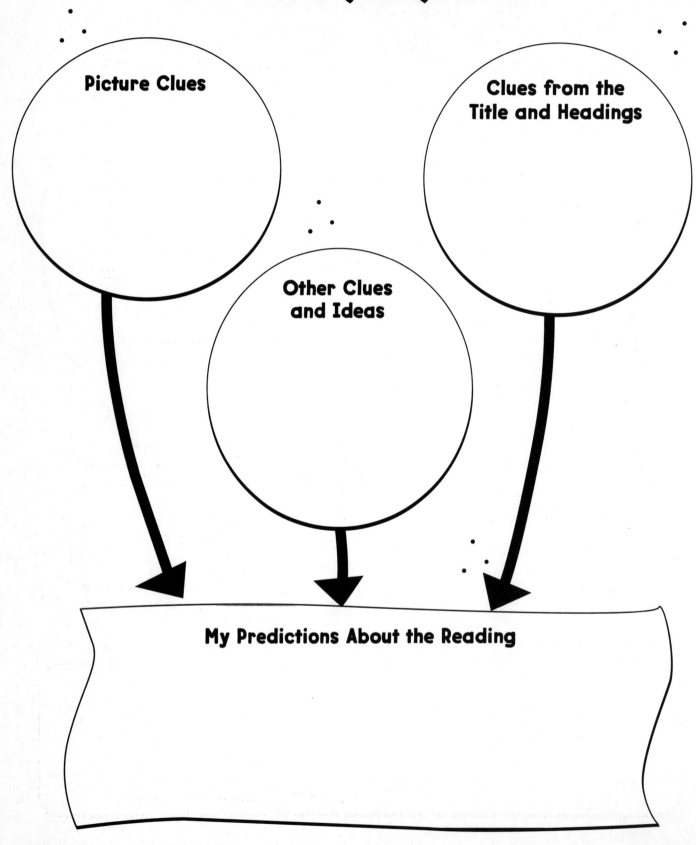

Picture Clues

Clues from the Title and Headings

Other Clues and Ideas

My Predictions About the Reading

Teaching Students to Read Nonfiction, Grades 2–4

Word Map

The word is . . .

It is not like . . .

It is like . . .

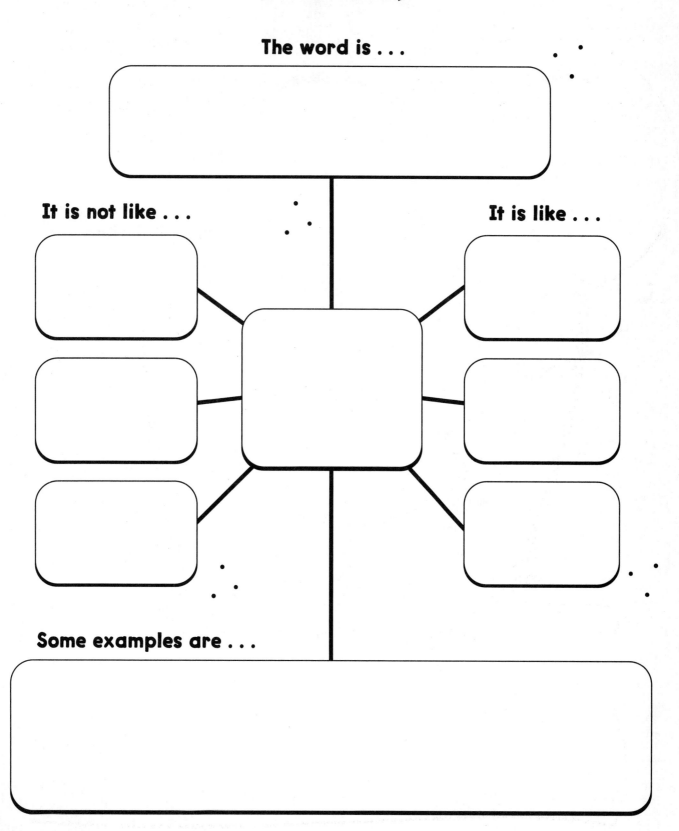

Some examples are . . .

Problem and Solution

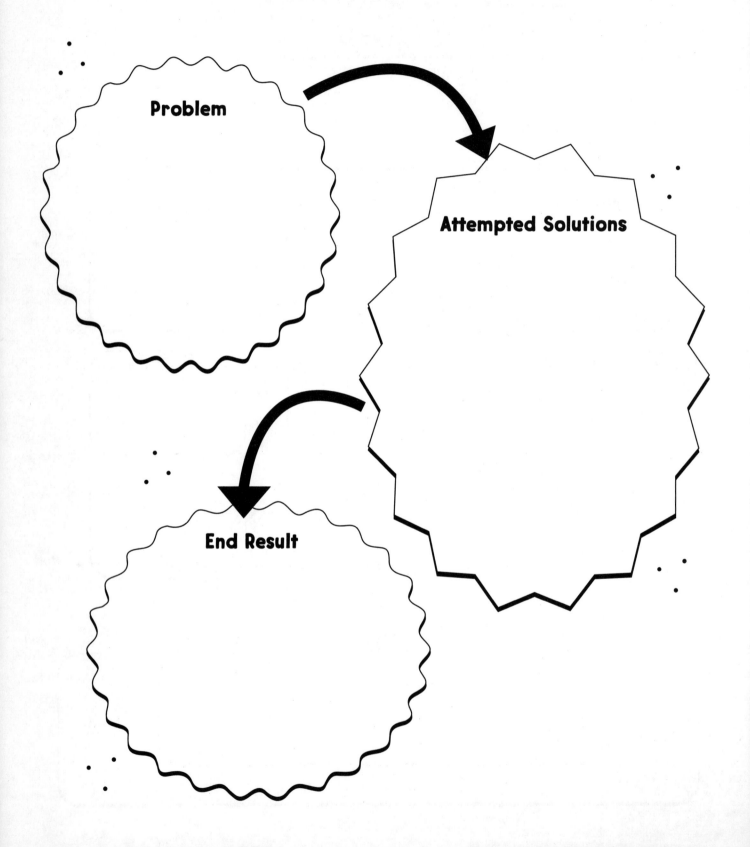

Problem

Attempted Solutions

End Result

Teaching Students to Read Nonfiction, Grades 2–4

Sequence Chart

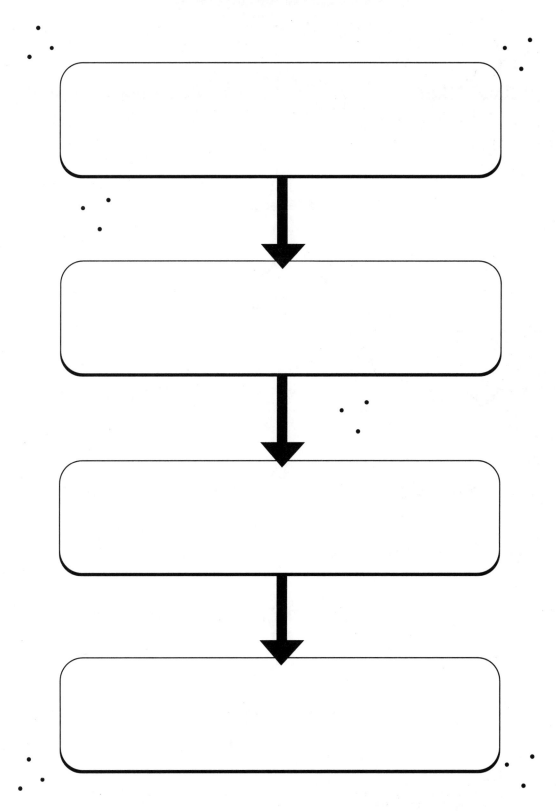

Compare Chart

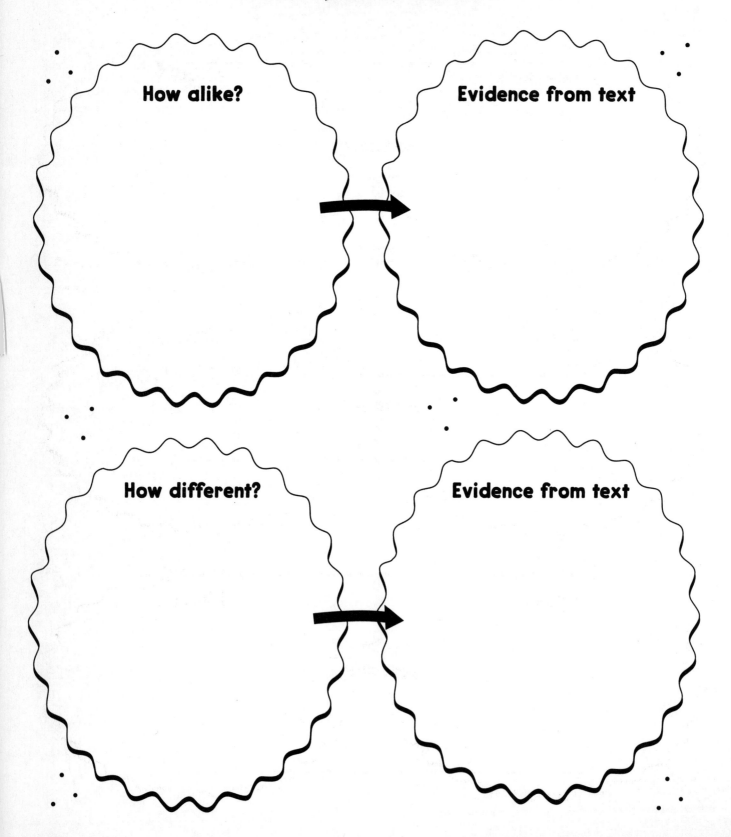

How alike?

Evidence from text

How different?

Evidence from text

Cause and Effect

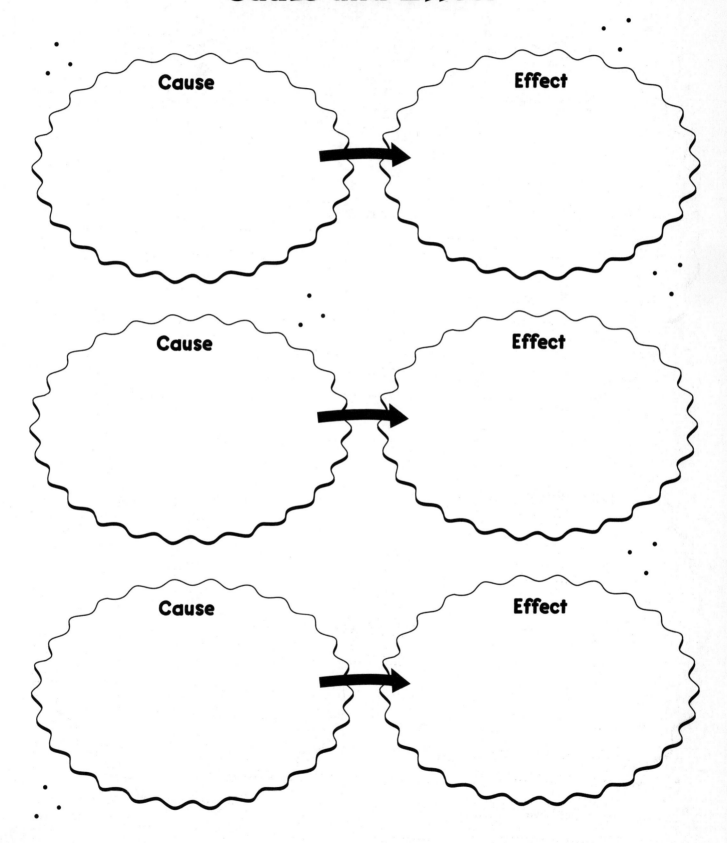

Cause → Effect

Cause → Effect

Cause → Effect

Capturing Context Clues

Word _____

page ___

What clue(s) from the text helped you figure out this word?

Your definition:

Dictionary definition:

What type of context clue is given?

☐ Restatement

☐ Compare/contrast

☐ Definition within text

Word _____

page ___

What clue(s) from the text helped you figure out this word?

Your definition:

Dictionary definition:

What type of context clue is given?

☐ Restatement

☐ Compare/contrast

☐ Definition within text